Praise for *The Wholehearted Life*

"I revel in the Heartfulness of Susyn's creation. *The Wholehearted Life* is a book to be cherished, savored, devoured...

Susyn's point of view is a beautiful tapestry of personal experience and practical wisdom, a hallmark of the exquisite romance between human and divine. She speaks with utter devotion to the intuitive knowing, joyfulness and bliss residing in all of us, and gently invites it, each day, with each page, to come play. Her words are ignited with her very heartbeat, so that we, in turn, can hear the rhythm of our own sacred song. I cherish Susyn's willingness to be so generously herself. And I thank her, with all my heart, for creating something so beautiful, and with such vigor, and love."

—Tatyana von Knobelsdorff,
author of *I Am the Sigh of a Woman Well Pleased: The Autobiography of Love's Evolution as Woman*

"Susyn Reeve gives us a map to peace and happiness—to truly BE peace and happiness. With her guidance this is possible, no matter what your situation may be. Allow this marvelous book to show you the way."

—Sandy Vilas,
CEO of CoachInc.com and author of *Power Networking*

D0150617

the
whole-
hearted
life

the whole-hearted life

big changes and greater happiness week by week

by susyn reeve

foreword by janet conner

Published in the United States by Viva Editions, an imprint of Cleis Press, Inc., 2246 Sixth Street, Berkeley, California 94710.

Printed in the United States.
Cover design: Scott Idleman/Blink
Cover photograph: iStockphoto
Text design: Frank Wiedemann

First Edition.
10 9 8 7 6 5 4 3 2 1

Trade paper ISBN: 978-1-936740-90-1
E-book ISBN: 978-1-63228-002-2

Library of Congress Cataloging-in-Publication Data

Reeve, Susyn.
 The wholehearted life : big changes and greater happiness week by week / Susyn Reeve. -- First edition.
     pages cm
 ISBN 978-1-936740-90-1 (paperback) -- ISBN 978-1-63228-002-2 (ebk)
 1. Peace of mind. 2. Happiness. 3. Conduct of life. 4. Spiritual life. I. Title.
 BF637.P3R443 2014
 158.1--dc23
                                    2014014061

To Maya, the daughter of my heart.

And to each person
committed to being a mighty expression
of Love in the world,
this book is dedicated to you.

table of contents

Foreword by Janet Conner xiii

Acknowledgments—Thanks, Thanks, Thanks xv

Introduction—Letter to Readers xvii

How to Use This Book xxiii

Prayer for Wholehearted Living xxx

Week 1. Use the Law of Attraction 1

Week 2. Breathe 11

Week 3. Have a New Thought—Be a New You 19

Week 4. Smile 25

Week 5. Use the Creative Power of Your Word 29

Week 6. Commit First 35

Week 7. Smell the Flowers 41

Week 8. Take a New Path 45

Week 9. Create a Daily Ritual 53

Week 10. Sing 59

Week 11. Live Your Dreams 63

Week 12. Eliminate Gossip 69

Week 13. Live Life as a Thank-You 73

Week 14. Write Your Obituary 77

Week 15. Spend Time with a Friend 81

Week 16. Write Down Your Soul 85

Week 17. Adorn Yourself. 91

Week 18. Acknowledge Accomplishments 101

Week 19. Meditate. 107

Week 20. Be a Visitor in Your Town 113

Week 21. Hug. 119

Week 22. Be Kind 125

Week 23. Live Abundantly 133

Week 24. Express Your Love 141

Week 25. Go on a Media Diet 145

Week 26. Listen to and Follow the Still Small Voice . . .151

Week 27. Use the Good Dishes 159

Week 28. Exercise Your Body and Your Mind. 165

Week 29. Use Your Feelings as Your Guide. 171

Week 30. Read Inspiring Words 179

Week 31. Take a Risk 185

Week 32. Ask for Help 191

Week 33. Be Forgiving 199

Week 34. Spend Time with a Pet. 209

Week 35. Seize the Moment—Be Here Now 215

Week 36. Experience the Power of Movies. 223

Week 37. Do Your Best 229

Week 38. Give Compliments. 235

Week 39. Ignite the Full Resources of Your Imagination. . 239

Week 40. Pray 247

Week 41. Detach and Let Go 255

Week 42. Eat Dessert First 265

Week 43. Be Silent 269

Week 44. Take a Vacation 273

Week 45. Listen to Music 279

Week 46. Spend Time with a Child 285

Week 47. Pamper Yourself 291

Week 48. Wake Up to Your Faith 295

Week 49. Harness the Power of Your Imagination . . . 303

Week 50. Enjoy a Massage 309

Week 51. Be the World's Greatest Lover 315

Week 52. Celebrate Success 321

Putting It All Together—Creating a Bag of Tricks . . . 327

Afterword 333

Resources 337

Permissions 341

About Susyn 343

Foreword

What is a wholehearted life? I knew I couldn't write this foreword until I could answer this question. But as I asked it of myself the first few times, I realized, oh, wait a minute, this is one of *those* questions—one of those big, deep, soul-activating questions that, once asked, will not leave us alone. And a quick superficial answer that might have once put smug, self-satisfied smiles on our faces will no longer do. The soul wants to know: *What is a wholehearted life?*

I picked up my soul-writing journal and wrote across the top of a page: "What is a wholehearted life?" The answer was swift: "When I live a wholehearted life, all of me shows up: all my love, all my desires, all my gifts, my strengths, my service, my energy, all my courage, and, yes, even all my weaknesses and fears. I am present—not little Janet, big Janet—the whole me, the human me, the divine me, the heart me, the soul me; all of me is present."

I thought that was a pretty good answer, but as so often happens in soul writing, the answer just triggered another question: *Why does a wholehearted life matter?* Oh, I thought, now there's an important question. The answer surprised me a bit: "Your heart is yours, but not only yours. You belong to the whole. Your whole heart is not just for you; it is in service to all. When you show up with your whole heart, you are a conduit for the great heart, the one heart, the only heart, and you heal the world."

Oh my. Suddenly Susyn Reeve's book felt truly holy in my hands. I always ask myself when I write a book or read a book, "Does this matter?" And the answer for *The Wholehearted Life* is clearly, "Yes, oh yes, oh yes."

I thought I was finished on the page, but one final question popped up: *How can we live a wholehearted life?* I laughed. Susyn Reeve has the *how* covered! Fifty-two weeks of how. Three hundred sixty-five days of little digestible nuggets of how. But don't take my word for it. Dive into this book and discover for yourself what happens when your wholehearted self begins to show up.

Janet Conner
author of *Writing Down Your Soul, The Lotus and The Lily,* and *Soul Vows: Gathering the Presence of the Divine in You, Through You, and as You*

Acknowledgments—
Thanks, Thanks, Thanks

The whole of my heart is filled with gratitude for my family, friends, colleagues, and the strangers whose wholehearted Love, support, expertise, and presence contributed to the birth and blossoming of this book.

To my wonderful friends who opened their homes to me, providing me loving writing sanctuaries in heavenly settings: Calla Crafts and Fred Finch, Eve Eliot, Suzi Higgins, Drew and Lynn Neidorf, and June Umanoff and Bo Parsons.

To the people who believe in me over and over and over again, and whose Love gives me the courage to be the best me and express that through the words on the pages of this book: Maya and Kevin Baker, David Rattiner, Robin and Mark Neiman, Lorraine Simone, Sheryl Hastalis, Ryan Weiss, Josie Thompson, Lynn Geiger, Rikk Hansen, Lisa Carvill, and *The Ladies*— Calla Crafts, Johanna Chase, and Judith Noel (thirty-five years, and counting, of pajama parties!).

This book would not have been possible without the extraordinary team at Viva Editions. Brenda Knight, you are the publisher that an author dreams of. Your commitment to allowing me to express myself so authentically and to midwife a beautiful book was priceless.

Felice Newman, Kara Wuest, Sara Giusti, and Eileen Duhné, my heart is happy that you are my Viva cheerleaders. And of course, Elizabeth Smith for your superb copyediting and Scott Idleman for a cover design that warms my heart.

Janet Conner, that you made the time in the midst of completing the editing of your new book to write the foreword for this book is something I will forever be grateful for. Thank you for clearly writing down the soul and capturing the very heart of this book.

I have a depth of gratitude to the public libraries in East Hampton, New York, and Hampton Bays, New York. I have loved libraries since I was six years old and was able to print my name clearly enough to get my first library card. When the distractions of my office were vying for my attention, these libraries were the antidote.

I am eternally grateful to The Thought Spiritual Community of Eastern Long Island. Thank you for all the ways you support me. A special heartfelt hug of gratitude goes to Nick Rutherford, who invited me to speak and deliver the Sunday message four years ago.

A very special thanks to my grandchildren, Solange and Rhone Baker. Your presence encourages me to be a mighty expression of Love in the world—which is really what this book is about.

Introduction—
Letter to Readers

Dear, dear *Reader*,

I've written this book as a present for you. As I step into the honored role of being a new Elder, filled with the wisdom of sixty-five years of life experience, I am eager to share what I have learned—both through personal experience and through the experiences of the thousands of people I have had the privilege of meeting and working with during my life, up 'til now.

This book reflects my growth and evolution—to continually deepen and expand my capacity to be, give, and receive *love*. I believe that living a life of passion and purpose requires a conscious choice—the choice to live a wholehearted life. To live with an open heart—a heart that has weathered storms; a heart that has been broken and through its cracks invites the healing light of Love in and allows its Loving light to shine through; a heart that continues to be nourished through the Love, Gratitude, and Joy of a life fully lived.

Living a wholehearted life is a reflection of the sacred union of our heart, mind, and body joined and aligned in conscious action. A wholehearted life is the evolution in consciousness that calls to each of us when we courageously allow ourselves to *be ourselves* and live an authentic life of passion and purpose; to acknowledge and share our unique gifts, talents, and skills; to know—to *grok*—that the challenges we have faced, the hardships and pain we have experienced, contain the seeds of greater compassion, love, and kindness. A wholehearted life is rooted in awareness that conscious connection matters more than anything—connection with the God of our understanding, connection with ourselves, connection with our purpose in this lifetime, and connection with one another—and a deep knowing that we are One.

When my professional life began after graduate school in 1973, I didn't yet have the deep appreciation that I now have for the gifts of the pain, struggles, and challenges we each face in life. While our personal circumstances—our personal histories—may appear to be different from one another, we are all born whole—fully aligned in body mind spirit. And we all have a story of being cast out of this garden of wholeness—our personal Garden of Eden.

In the Old Testament it is the story of Adam and Eve. Adam was told that he could eat from all the trees in the garden except the tree of knowledge of good and evil. If he were to eat the fruit of this tree, he would be banished from the garden—heaven on earth—and surely die, not a physical death, but rather a death of his connection with God and of the experience of being whole. This is the separation we experience: the disconnection of our higher Self and ego mind; the separation of our inner and outer experience; the disconnection of our heart, mind, and body. This casting out of the garden may occur at the hands of horrific trauma—physical, psychological, emotional, sexual—or it may occur when you are compared to a sibling who got higher grades on a report card.

Whatever the cause of this disconnection, the result is an experience of *I'm not enough*—a barrage of self-talk: *I'm not pretty enough, thin enough, handsome enough, successful enough, worthy enough, lovable enough.* The list goes on and on and on; even *I'm too much!* is really a version of *I'm not enough: I'm too much for others to handle, too intense, too dramatic, too self-involved, too sensitive.* We judge and demonize others, projecting our *not enough*ness onto them: *He's evil. She's stupid. They don't deserve what they have.*

Our journey in life is to heal this rift of separation—to come home to being whole. It is important to remember that it is a journey. There is no destination where, once you arrive, you will never experience discomfort, disappointment, sadness, or anger. Rather, there is the understanding that these challenges, these experiences of being brokenhearted, are growing pains and truly a call for us to deepen, expand, and evolve our capacity to be, give, and receive love—to allow love to flow in and out and through us—to be wholehearted.

Here's the story I have made up about life: We choose to enroll in Earth School to learn to be, give, and receive love. Each one of us is born with the seeds of our personal purpose within us, just as the coding of a mighty oak is present in an acorn. The lessons quickly begin, and we forget the *calling* that is the reason we enrolled in this university. As we learn about life on Earth, we begin to embody the current agreed-upon thinking. For many centuries the prevalent thought was that there was a separation between our inner and outer world, between our body mind spirit, between our thoughts and our experience. But this is only one point of view—throughout the ages, indigenous cultures as well as the spiritual foundations of all religions have believed in the interconnectedness of all Life. I have always found the following words of Chief Seattle, who lived from 1780–1866 and was the chief of the Duwamish tribe, to be a potent reminder of the interrelatedness of all beings.

> *The earth does not belong to man, man belongs to the earth. All things are connected like the blood that unites us all. Man did not weave the web of life, he is merely a strand in it. Whatever he does to the web, he does to himself.*
>
> —CHIEF SEATTLE

As we begin to see and experience the world through our beliefs—learned from the significant people in our lives, the current zeitgeist, the media, and authorities—we act as though those beliefs are truth. We go through life in a trance, continually repeating patterns of thought and behavior on automatic—like a default setting on our computers. We have wake-up calls that may, at first, be gentle, yet when not tended to get louder and louder and louder in the form of *ouch*es—health problems, relationship struggles, career setbacks, financial woes, spiritual crises, addictions, and ongoing fear and anxiety. In the presence of these threats we often feel victimized and use these hardships as evidence that there is something wrong with us; that life is against us and we are being punished. At the same time, each life struggle offers a key to open our hearts and minds to a new possibility—a willingness to explore the gift that the hardship contains.

In my experience, I've noticed that my initial reaction to heartbreak is to feel victimized. Now, after decades of learning to wake up to the sensations in my body, I now know what isolation, pain, and suffering physically feel like (a wrenching sensation in my stomach, sleepless nights, unquenchable hunger) and in my thoughts (obsessing over the past; worrying what other people think of me; feeling confused, uncertain, and scared to express my thoughts). As soon as I notice that I am in the midst of a drama where I have cast myself in the role of victim, I acknowledge what I'm feeling, take a deep breath, and ask myself two simple questions: *What is the gift here? What would love do here?*

This practice of acknowledgment, and directing my attention and curiosity to these questions, opens my heart and mind to listen and be awake to a new perspective. I remember that I am a co-creative partner with a loving God; I believe that every experience is an expression of Love or a call for Love, and I allow the gifts to be revealed. I allow myself to surrender to the loving energy of the universe that always responds with a resounding *Yes* to the thoughts that are the dominant creative force in my experience—the thoughts that I am embodying and aligned within body mind spirit, the thoughts that I have faith in. I remember that my Earth School curriculum is to be a mighty expression of Love in the world.

So, dear Reader, I have filled this book with the small steps that you can easily take each and every day that will lead to big changes in your life. I know the power of consistent, regular practice, and I know the joys of living a wholehearted life. Wherever you are in your personal experience, a life of purpose, passion, and love is your birthright.

With wholehearted appreciation for your commitment to being a mighty expression of Love in the world,

Susyn

How to Use This Book

This book was written to be used over the course of a year, allowing you to experiment with different points of view and practices in order to install a software upgrade in your mind, create a personal ritual that nourishes wholehearted living in your daily life, and stock your personal medicine bag with remedies, tools, charms, and reminders to continually expand your capacity for wholehearted living.

The book consists of fifty-two ideas, one for each week of the year. Each wholehearted idea then has seven days of exercises, one for each day of the week. Day 7 is a weekly reflection, which you can do in a journal, a computer document, or even as a video recording. Some people love having a clear structure and will easily follow the exercises in the order they are given. Others may prefer to choose the order for themselves, and may even skip some exercises. What is most important is to practice and experiment with the exercises described.

I suggest that rather than simply reading the book from cover to cover, you take the time to digest its wisdom. Combine the reading with the daily practices in service of aligning yourself in body mind spirit to being wholehearted. Being able to talk the talk is ultimately ineffective if you are not walking the walk.

Wholehearted living requires action and repetition in order to lead from your heart, create upgraded software and brain pathways, and be and act as an expression of love. Being wholehearted, and living life as though every moment is an expression of love, involves both having a conceptual understanding of the ideas involved *and* putting them into action in your daily life. With this in mind, here are three ways to use this book. Choose one, or use the combination that works best for you.

The simplest way is to start at the beginning and focus on one chapter per week. Do one exercise each day, and work your way through the entire book over the course of a year.

If you prefer a less structured approach, choose an intention to guide you. Before opening the book, narrow your focus for the day by consciously declaring a clear intention. Then, open the book at random, read some or all of the chapter, choose an exercise to do, and reflect on how this lesson relates to your intention. Here are examples of intentions to focus on:

- I choose my highest guidance to expand my capacity to be _____. (Fill in the blank with the quality you want to explore. For instance, you may choose to be forgiving, patient, loving, playful, sexy, disciplined, accepting, sensuous, joyful, etc.)
- Guide me in how best to deal with _____ _____. (Identify a challenging circumstance or relationship to resolve.)
- Show me my next step to achieve _____. (Identify a specific dream, goal, or result you are committed to.)

Finally, if you'd like to share your journey with others, you can use the book in a mastermind group in which you share ideas and support one another in bringing your dreams to life. Invite family or friends to meet weekly, or if you lead personal development groups as part of your work, form a group using this book as the text and workbook for your meetings. Here is a sample structure for each ninety minute session.

1. Begin the session by saying the *Prayer for Whole-hearted Living* (page xxx).

2. Move onto guided visualization centering (the "be here now technique"): If you want to listen along, here is the mp3 link on my website: http://susynreeve.com/videos-and-audios.

To begin, write down all the things that are cluttering your mind right now. Include chores to complete, concerns, and questions you have. As you write each item down, know that you are clearing your mind to be more fully present here and now. When your list is complete, put it down and:

- Sit comfortably and close your eyes.
- Focus your attention on your breath and prepare to count from one to five. Inhale a sense of calm and relaxation through your nose and then exhale completely through your mouth.
- At the end of your count of five, you will experience yourself as more relaxed and at ease, ready to expand your experience of confidence and well being in the present moment.
- *One*: Pay attention to your breathing while you

inhale a sense of serenity and relaxation, and exhale fully.

- *Two*: If you notice any tension or tightness, breathe into that part of your body. As you exhale, experience yourself as more relaxed and more at ease.
- *Three*: If thoughts enter your mind, simply notice them. As you exhale, let them go. Continue to focus your attention on your breath—breathe in a deeper sense of calm and exhale completely.
- *Four*: Allow yourself to fully relax your mind and body. Feel a sense of confidence and renewal filling your being.
- And *five*: Experience yourself as relaxed, alert, and self-assured. Experience your body as fully supported by the seat beneath you. Let peace, happiness, and confidence fill your being as you open yourself to deepening your experience of those emotions.
- Now, as you are fully present in this moment, slowly and effortlessly allow your eyes to open. Focus on feeling wide awake, alert and better than before.

3. Identify norms and ground rules. For example:

- Start and end on time.
- Let someone know if you will miss a particular session and get and complete the assignment for the next session.
- Do the reading and experiment with the exercises.
- One person speaks at a time.

- Give advice to others only if you are directly asked for it.
- Keep the focus on the sensations you experience in your body, your thought and behavior patterns, and how they contribute to or detract from a wholehearted life; not on how other people *should* be different or are the cause of your problems. This is keeping the first attention on yourself.
- If asked, support one another in identifying patterns of thought and behavior. Don't give advice to fix them or get seduced by the drama of or your identification with the story they are telling.
- Ask for and allow help when you need it.
- Have fun.

4. At your first group meeting, have group members share why they are joining the group, focusing on what they want. For example: *As a result of living a wholehearted life, I have a book contract. As a result of living a wholehearted life, my relationship with my children is loving, fun, and satisfying for all of us. Through my active participation in this group, my relationship with money has transformed—I always have enough to share and enough to spare. Through my commitment to a wholehearted life, I appreciate all the gifts in my life.*

5. During future group meetings, go around in a circle and respond to the following items:

- Describe your most powerful *wholehearted life* experience since we last met.

- What was your experience with the exercises?
- How are you going to continue to use this idea in your daily life?

Note: Have a clear time frame for the check-in at the beginning of each group meeting (for instance, fifteen minutes for all group members to share) or you may notice that suddenly an hour has gone by. While it is important to use a structure, if there is a topic that generates a strong reaction and conversation you may decide to focus on it. If you do, ask the members of the group whether focusing on the issue that has come up would be most helpful to them now. (Stories can be very seductive and can take a long time to tell. Remember: As a listener, your focus is to identify patterns of thought, feelings, and behavior—not to get lost in the details of a personal drama!)

---

6. Read the chapter you are focusing on this week aloud. You can have one person read it, or have each person read a paragraph—experiment! I highly recommend that each person read the week's material before the group meets.

7. Identify one person in the group to be the leader for the discussion. The leader will prepare questions that relate to the chapter and may also generate a list of resources. It is empowering for everyone in the group to step into

the role of the leader. Here are some sample questions:

- What is your understanding of this idea?
- How does this idea contribute to a wholehearted life?
- Do you currently practice this idea? If so, how?
- What challenges do you anticipate in practicing this idea?
- What support do you need to practice it anyway?

8. Choose the chapter and leader for the next session. (You may decide to follow the chapters in order, or have the leader for the next week choose the chapter, or open to the Table of Contents and randomly choose a topic.)

9. End the group with the *Prayer for Wholehearted Living* (page xxx).

Are you wondering where to begin? Begin here, with a prayer, an intention, declaring your commitment to living a wholehearted life.

Prayer for Wholehearted Living

Today, I live a wholehearted life. I easily let go of my attachment to thoughts and behaviors that block the in-flow and out-flow of Love in my life. I know my purpose is to be a mighty expression of Love in the world through my unique gifts, talents, and skills. I trust that every experience I have is an opportunity to deepen and expand my capacity to be, give, and receive Love. I ask for and receive all help available to me, visible and invisible, to effortlessly learn from and release habit patterns of fear, blame, and separation, to have faith in a loving future, and to live fully and wholeheartedly in the present.

To the Eternal Peace and Happiness of All.

And, so it is.

WEEK 1
Use the Law of Attraction

There seems to be a great law of Nature whereby an atom attracts to itself that which is needed for its development. And the force that brings about these results manifests itself in Desire. There may be many Desires, but the predominant one has the strongest attracting power. This law is recognized through the various kingdoms of Nature, but it is only beginning to be realized that the same Law maintains in the kingdom of the mind.

—WILLIAM WALKER ATKINSON
FROM *THE LAW OF NEW THOUGHT*, 1902

The Law of Attraction, which became popular through movies such as *The Secret*, *What the Bleep Do We Know*, and is evident in *Groundhog Day*, and through books by Esther and Jerry Hicks, is actually a universal law that is at the foundation of the spiritual principles of all major religious traditions. This universal law has been proven by quantum physics, and written about in many books, including *The Biology of Belief* by Bruce Lipton.

Understanding the Law of Attraction is key to understanding the creative process and living a whole-hearted life. This is not simply a trendy New Age idea. That the Law of Attraction is now part of mainstream conversation is an expression of the ongoing and ever-evolving expansion of consciousness. It is the first lesson in this book because it is a tool that operates in your life, whether or not you are aware of it. Being awake to how it works, and using it consciously, opens the door to heaven on earth.

The Law of Attraction is actually quite simple to understand: What you think is what you get. Thoughts fueled with desire (emotional energy), spoken with authority (you are the author!), and acted on with conviction (faith) are what you create in your life.

This law operates whether or not you are conscious of your thoughts. It is as if the universe, the greater field of life, hears you through your dominant thoughts—your energetic vibration—and always responds with one verse (a uni-verse)—a resounding YES. This means that all of your life experience begins through you. Every-thing, every relationship, every event, is first created in your consciousness before it takes form in three-dimen-sional reality. Each of us is continuously creating our world. Consciously using this knowledge is a point of great power.

To shift your point of view, transform your beliefs, and upgrade the software of your mind to align with your heart's desire—your Calling and dreams—requires commitment and discipline, the same kind of discipline and focus necessary to train for a marathon. Left to our own devices, most of us are lazy, tending to follow the path of least resistance—the patterns of thinking and behavior we follow on automatic—whether or not that path is satisfying.

If you desire a deeper and more consistent experi-ence of peace and happiness in your life, then your dominant thoughts must reflect this desire. Often when we have a strong desire for something, we are used to *looking* to see if it is there yet. Embedded in this *looking* is the belief that it isn't there (since if it were there, we wouldn't be looking for it!). We are so used to giving more power to visible outside circumstances than to the power of our invisible intention wedded with faith that we often simply don't allow the infinite gifts available to us into our lives.

A crucial stumbling block to living a wholehearted life is that many of us—certainly everyone I have ever met—are walking around with beliefs about ourselves that go something like this:

- I'm not good enough.
- I'm not kind enough.
- I'm not smart enough.
- I'm not wealthy enough.
- I'm not strong enough.
- I'm not young enough.
- I'm not thin enough.
- I'm not lovable enough.
- I'm not worthy enough.

We have gathered so much evidence through the years to support these beliefs that we have unwavering faith in them, and the Law of Attraction goes into high gear, saying *yes* to our dominant thoughts. Thereby we view the circumstances we encounter through the filter of these beliefs, continuing to get what we don't want.

Rather than deciding whether you believe or don't believe in the Law of Attraction, I invite you to act as if it is true. Imagine it is true, and play with it. If some evidence would help you, think of all those situations you have called coincidence or synchronicity—for example, when you think of someone and they seem to call you out of the blue, or when you hear about a new book, movie, or app that you'd never heard of before and suddenly the next person you talk with mentions it as well. Or you say you are certain you are not going to get a parking space in the center of town and you don't; or you meet someone and you know within moments that this is the person you'll marry, and now you are married to that person. The truth is that the Law of Attraction has been operating in your life already.

What if you are truly made in the image of the Creator and you are the artist, the creator of the greatest masterpiece of all: your life? Would you choose heaven rather than hell, peace rather than war, love rather than fear? Make these choices this week and every day and notice peace and happiness taking center stage in your life.

How to Do It

Day 1: Play with the Law of Attraction. Focus on things and people and watch them show up. Imagine loose change in the morning and then spend thirty seconds pretending it is the end of the day and you are telling your family and friends that you found loose change today. Then let it go. Release this idea into the universe like a helium balloon. During the day, loose change will have your name on it. There's no telling where it will show up: on the street, in your car ashtray that you haven't opened since you first got the car, in your raincoat pocket, inside your wallet. Whenever it shows up, acknowledge it by saying, *"Yes, the Law of Attraction works."* The universe, your co-creative partner, will say YES to this idea as well. Play. This format may be helpful:

- Identify something you want to attract.
- Imagine you've attracted it. Create a virtual reality, and for thirty seconds, visualize your desire realized. Make sure to include yourself in the picture and how you feel achieving your results—getting out of your car after easily pulling into a perfect parking space, saying to yourself, *"It was really easy getting this space"* and feeling great about it with a smile on your face; or sitting in a seat immediately after boarding a crowded bus, thinking, *"I'm so glad I got this seat"* and feeling relaxed and at ease.
- Let it go. Allow the universe to conspire with you to provide and guide you.
- Receive it when it knocks at your door.
- Allow and acknowledge it.

Day 2: Identify what is in your life that is not a source of peace and happiness, and focus your attention on what you do want. For example, if your job is unsatisfying and you have spent much of the past six months complaining about it, stop the complaining and imagine you are in a satisfying job. If creating a virtual reality with your boss in it results in anxious feelings, imagine that you are getting home from work and telling your family or friends what a great day you had at work. Allow the universe to provide the details. You may unexpectedly get a call from a headhunter with a great job for you to interview for; your boss may be transferred and your new boss is great—or maybe you are offered that position! Have faith that the universe has heard you and let it go. And if all thoughts about work result in feelings of unrest, trust that the universe has heard your desire for a satisfying job and instead focus your attention on something that gives you pleasure, because that is the vibration that allows you to be open to the resounding *yes* of the universe responding to your desire.

Day 3: Any time during the day that you are out of sync with peace and happiness, choose, in the moment, to attract a new experience. Here's how to do it:

- Acknowledge that you are feeling yucky. You have been seduced by abusive and judgmental thoughts about yourself or others. You are feeling victimized and isolated. Revenge may be on your mind, or perhaps guilt has found a comfortable home!
- Say "Oops." Use your personal power to stop the train of sabotaging thoughts.
- Choose your desire. Say aloud (allowed!) or think to yourself: "I choose to feel (happy, light-hearted, grateful, etc.)."
- Let it go and move on. With your attention focused in the present moment, smell the flowers and enjoy the precious present.

Day 4: Make a Pleasure List of the people, places, things, and activities that generate an experience of pleasure for you. Carry the list with you and put it where you can see it—on your smartphone or computer, pasted to your refrigerator, or by the side of your bed. Use this list to shift your attention when you are feeling victimized by life. Here are some of my Pleasure List items:

- The sound of my grandkids' giggles.
- The morning sun glistening on the ocean as I walk along the water's edge, my dog playfully romping ahead of me.
- Snuggling with my lover on the couch in front of a roaring fire.
- Getting a massage.
- The full moon lighting up the sky.
- A bowl of delicious soup on a cold, rainy winter day.
- Hearing the sound of my golf club connect with the ball and seeing the ball soar and land on the green on a glorious fall afternoon.

Day 5: Use the Law of Attraction for the well-being of others. Here are some ways to do this:

- If you have a family member or friend who has been suffering, place his or her photo somewhere you can easily see it. Every time you look at the photo, see him as whole and happy; say a prayer for her highest good.
- If you pass a car accident on the road, instead of getting caught up in the horror, say a prayer for the well-being of all involved and express your gratitude for the emergency service workers who are assisting. I have noticed that when I do this, rather than getting seduced by the drama, I feel as if I am contributing to the well-being of the people involved as well as my own well-being.

Day 6: Expand the Law of Attraction to the world. See peace on earth. Imagine a newscaster declaring peace in places where there is strife. Use the power of your thoughts to influence the collective consciousness of the planet. What we focus our attention on expands. This is true in our individual lives, in our families, communities, workplaces, countries, and in the world.

Day 7: Reflect and write your response to the following questions:

- What did you learn about the Law of Attraction?
- What did you learn about yourself in relation to the Law of Attraction?
- How can you consciously apply the Law of Attraction in your daily life? Do it.

Loose Change

When I wrote this chapter, the idea to practice the Law of Attraction with loose change simply popped into my mind as I wrote the Day 1 exercise. The next morning, I went to the gym. When I got on the elliptical trainer to work out, there was loose change in the cup holder. The Law of Attraction popped into my mind and I smiled. After thirty minutes, I got off the elliptical trainer and went to another section of the gym to lift free weights. After a few minutes, I realized that I'd left my newfound loose change where I had found it. When I finished using the weights, as I bent down to pick up my towel, I saw more loose change. "Ah, yes," I thought, "when I express a desire and let it go, the universe says: Yes."

> Ask, and it will be given to you;
> Seek, and you will find;
> Knock, and it will be opened to you.
> —MATTHEW 7:7

WEEK 2
Breathe

> The practice of mindful breathing may be very simple, but the effect can be great. Focusing on our in-breath, we release the past, we release the future, we release our projects. We ride on that breath with all our being. Our mind comes back to our body, and we are truly there, alive, in the present moment. We are home.
>
> —THICH NHAT HANH

Breathe. Breath is life. Consciously focusing your attention on your breath is the most powerful and potent natural resource you have for being awake in the present moment.

Right now, stop for a moment and turn your attention to your in-breath and out-breath.

Do this five times. What do you notice? Are you more aware of your body? Are you feeling quieter? I notice that when I focus my attention on my breath—actually following the path of my breath as it enters my body through my nose, circulates throughout my body, and leaves my body through my mouth—I feel a deeper sense of relaxation and calm, and am more fully present in the moment. This is the power of focusing on your breath.

Our most basic common link is that we all inhabit this small planet.
We all breathe the same air.

—JOHN F. KENNEDY

We are connected with all beings, all that is, through our breath. We are inhaling one another's exhale all the time. Although it looks as if we are separated from others by the space between our bodies and the objects of our world, we are actually connected through our breath. As you exhale, your breath is charged with the emotional frequency of the thoughts you are thinking at that moment. Your emotional frequency, in each moment, contributes to the collective consciousness with each exhalation. Thoughts are real things, and what you think therefore makes a very big impact in the world—you pass your thoughts around through your breath! What do you contribute to the world through your exhalations—love, fear, happiness, anxiety, heaven, or hell?

How to Do It

Day 1: Become aware of your breath. Create a *Breathe* screen saver on your smartphone, tablet, or computer. Put sticky notes around your house, workplace, and car as reminders to you to *Breathe*. When you see these reminders, stop and *Breathe*. Take full, deep breaths, using your diaphragm: when you inhale, your belly expands, and when you exhale, it contracts. Experiment with simply focusing on expanding and contracting your diaphragm, and notice how breath is automatically drawn into and expelled from your body; play with having your breath breathe you. Do a search on the web or in your local library or bookstore or ask a yoga teacher to give you suggestions to experiment with different breathing exercises.

Day 2: Meditate for at least ten minutes, focusing your attention on your breath. When your mind wanders, bring your attention back to your breath, your inhalation and exhalation.

Day 3: Meditate for at least ten minutes and focus on moving your breath through your entire body. Start at your feet: Inhale into your feet and feel your feet relax as you exhale. (To use your breath to enhance your body awareness even more, you can focus on one toe at a time; one finger at a time, etc... After each exhalation, focus your attention and breath on another body part: your knees, your ankles, your liver, your heart, your ears, your eyelids, your lips, etc.)

Day 4: Anytime your feel tension in your body, breathe into that part of your body, and as you exhale, allow the tension to leave your body and breathe it into the Earth. (The Earth has the powerful ability to take whatever is given to her and transform it into support and nourishment, as long as we also give her love and care.) You can also do this exercise when worrisome and fearful thoughts have captured your attention.

Day 5: Once an hour, for five consecutive breaths, imagine that God is gently blowing breath into your being and that each exhalation is your gift to the collective consciousness. One of the ways I play with this is on my morning beach walks: When the wind is blowing, I stand with my mouth open and allow the air to fill my body, and then, as I exhale, I give to the wind the air that is moving through my being.

Listen, are you breathing just a little and calling it a life?

—MARY OLIVER

Breathe. Let go. And remind yourself that this very moment is the only one you know you have for sure.

—OPRAH WINFREY

Feelings come and go like clouds in a windy sky. Conscious breathing is my anchor.

—THICH NHAT HANH

Fear less, hope more; eat less, chew more; whine less, breathe more; talk less, say more; hate less, love more; and all good things are yours.

—SWEDISH PROVERB

Day 6: Meditate for twenty minutes, following the instructions of Thich Nhat Hanh, a Buddhist monk, contemporary meditation teacher, and author:

> *Breathing in I calm my mind and body.*
> *Breathing out I smile.*
> *Breathing in I dwell in the moment.*
> *This is the only moment.*

Day 7: Reflect and write your response to the following questions:

- What have you learned this week by focusing your attention on your breath?
- How did focusing your attention on your breath contribute to greater peace of mind?
- How can you use your breath on a daily basis to nourish wholehearted living?

The Breath Is Life's Teacher

by Donna Martin

Observe me, says the Breath, and learn to live effortlessly in the Present Moment.
Feel me, says the Breath, and feel the Ebb and Flow of Life.
Allow me, says the Breath, and I'll sustain and nourish you, filling you with energy and cleansing you of tension and fatigue.

Move with me, says the Breath, and I'll invite your soul
to dance.
Make sounds with me and I shall teach your soul to sing.
Follow me, says the Breath, and I'll lead you out to
the farthest reaches of the Universe, and inward to the
deepest parts of your inner world.

Notice, says the Breath, that I am as valuable to you
coming or going...that every part of my cycle is as
necessary as another...that after I'm released, I return
again and again...that even after a long pause—
moments when nothing seems to happen—eventually I
am there.
Each time I come, says the Breath, I am a gift from
Life. And yet you release me without regret...without
suffering...without fear.
Notice how you take me in, invites the Breath. Is it
with joy...with gratitude...? Do you take me in fully...
invite me into all the inner spaces of your home? ...Or
carefully into just inside the door? What places in you
am I not allowed to nourish?

And notice, says the Breath, how you release me. Do
you hold me prisoner in closed up places in the body?
Is my release resisted...do you let me go reluctantly, or
easily?

And are my waves of Breath, of Life, as gentle as a
quiet sea, softly smoothing sandy stretches of yourself...? Or anxious, urgent, choppy waves...? Or the
crashing tumult of a stormy sea...?

And can you feel me as the link between your inner and outer worlds...feel me as Life's exchange between the Universe and You? The Universe breathes me into You... You send me back to the Universe. I am the flow of life between every single part and the Whole.

Your attitude to me, says the Breath, is your attitude to Life. Welcome me...embrace me fully. Let me nourish you completely, then set me free. Move with me, dance with me, sing with me, sigh with me... Love me. Trust me. Don't try to control me.

I am the Breath.
Life is the Musician.
You are the flute.
And music—creativity—depends on all of us. You are not the Creator...nor the Creation.
We are all a part of the process of Creativity...You, Life, and me: the Breath.

WEEK 3

Have a New Thought—
Be a New You

Thoughts held in mind, manifest over time.

—ERNEST HOLMES

Having a new thought is about consciously choosing where you place your attention. Since your thoughts are the seeds of the life you create and live, what you think is very important. Often people are asleep to their thoughts—the ones that run like a continuous tape of self-talk in their heads as well as the ones that they articulate. Have you ever looked at yourself in the mirror in the morning and thought with conviction, "I look awful"? This is a powerful example of self-abuse, and the moment you notice this abuse is the perfect time to have a new thought. This week your practice is twofold:

1. Become aware of your thoughts. It is a daunting task to pay attention to each and every thought. A simple approach is to pay attention to your feelings, the sensations in your body. When you are feeling good, check in with yourself and notice your thoughts. When you are feeling bad, victimized, unworthy, journeying on a one-way ticket to hell, ask yourself, "What am I thinking right now that is creating an experience of hell for me?"

2. Have a new thought when your thoughts are abusive and judgmental of yourself or others.

How to Do It

Day 1: Check in with yourself throughout the day and listen to your thoughts. When you wake in the morning, what are your first thoughts? When you are eating, what are you telling yourself? When you look at yourself in the mirror, what are your thoughts? As you travel to work; when you are with your spouse, children, friends, lover, coworkers; when you are waiting for an elevator, what are the thoughts you feed yourself? Are these thoughts an expression of love or fear, happiness or misery? You have the power in each and every moment to choose thoughts that generate peace of mind.

Day 2: Write down your beliefs. Remember, beliefs are thought habits—thoughts charged with emotional energy that you have thought repeatedly until you think they are true. What are your beliefs about yourself, love, romance, work, family, health, finances, peace on Earth, God, and so forth? Are your beliefs expressions of love? If not, have a new thought.

Day 3: Listen to yourself as you speak. Do your words support the wholehearted life you desire, or are they abusive and judgmental? If they are abusive and judgmental, consciously change them right there and then.

Day 4: Appreciate yourself for waking up from the trance of life on automatic and noticing your thoughts and words. It is important that you are self-accepting; otherwise you are reinforcing abusive and judgmental behavior. Whenever you notice your thoughts throughout the day, give yourself a pat on the back for your enhanced awareness.

Day 5: Make a list of thoughts that support the life you want to live. Some of the thoughts on my list are:

- I am love.
- Health and well-being are my daily experience.
- Everything I eat turns to health and beauty.
- I am abundant and financially prosperous.
- I am sexy and sensual.
- I am successful in my work.
- Everyone is an expression of God.

From this list, make signs to place around your home, office, and car as reminders of the thoughts you want to fill your life with—the thoughts you want to think often enough to create new brain pathways and a new set of beliefs.

Day 6: Since human beings are natural storytellers, much of the angst we experience is based on the stories we make up about our circumstances. When you realize you have the power to make up new stories, you can transform your life at any moment. I remember many years ago, when I participated in an est (Erhard Seminars Training) workshop, human beings were described as meaning-making machines. Today, play with making up multiple stories about the circumstances you experience. For instance, if your boss stops by your desk and asks you to come into her office, here are some possible thoughts you can have about it:

- Oh, she must want to compliment me on the project I just completed.
- There must be something important she wants to tell me.
- I wonder what I did wrong.
- Oh good, this will give me a chance to thank her for being flexible with my work schedule the past two days.

Knowing that we make up stories and choose our thoughts, choose to focus on thoughts that are supportive of heaven rather than falling into the trap of anticipating hell. This technique can even be applied to making up a new story about your past.

Day 7: Reflect and write your response to the following questions:

- What did you notice about your thoughts?
- What was the impact on your experience when you had a new thought?
- How did making up a new thought contribute to your open heartedness?

> The greatest discovery of our generation is that a human being can alter his life by altering his attitudes.
>
> —WILLIAM JAMES

WEEK 4

Smile

Sometimes your joy is the source of your smile, but
sometimes your smile can be the source of your joy.

—THICH NHAT HANH

Smiling is a simple, magical gesture that expresses peace
and happiness. It is a gift we can easily give. When we
give it away to others, we clearly receive the benefit of
the energy of the smile moving through us. I remember
hearing on a stress management video many years ago
that it takes seventeen muscles to smile and forty-three
to frown. So a smile requires much less effort than a
scowl—and in the words of a Ziggy cartoon, "A smile is
a face-lift that's in everyone's price range!"

I have noticed the power of a smile to change my
experience in the moment. Many years ago, in a
yoga class I was taking, the instructor, Ani Kalfayan,

would say, "Turn up the corners of your mouth. Yoga is meant to be joyful." I followed her instructions, and I immediately experienced a lightness of being. Smiles are clearly a happiness drug. I have also noticed the power of a smile when I am paying a cashier. Words may not even be exchanged, but magic happens in the moment. A connection is made, and the present moment becomes a precious present. I am also aware that I have another smile. It's the sourpuss smile, and behind this smile a judge is holding court—doling out judgments and communicating to others what I think I am hiding behind the smile.

> If you have only one smile in you, give it to the people you love. Don't be surly at home, then go out in the street and start grinning "Good morning" at total strangers.
>
> — MAYA ANGELOU

This week, get to know your smiles. Use your smiles to share your love; make them a gateway to transforming your experience from sad to glad. Play and smile and imagine all the love, kindness, and compassion you would experience each and every day if you let a smile light your way.

How to Do It

Day 1: Give away fifty smiles today. As a reminder, write *Smile* in bright letters on your calendar, on sticky notes that you put around your house, car, and workplace. Put it on your screen saver; leave yourself a voice mail message that says "*Smile.*"

Day 2: Smile to yourself fifty times today. When you are walking down the street and you notice a neutral expression or a frown on your face, *smile*. While you're in the shower, *smile*.

Day 3: Make a list of all the things and memories that bring a smile to your whole being when you think about them. Post the list somewhere you can see it. Five times today, look at your list, give your attention to it, and open your heart as a smile makes its way through you. This is a powerful practice of consciously choosing where to focus your attention. The more practice you have, the more easily you can access happy thoughts when you are flirting with drama. You are strengthening your happy thought muscle today.

Day 4: Every time you look in a mirror today, smile at yourself. A smile that says, "I'm glad to see you;" "I'm one handsome dude;" "I'm beautiful."

Day 5: Search the web for "smile quotations." Find ones that make you smile. Copy them and put them somewhere you can see them; put one in the bottom of your sock drawer so it pops out at you one day, at the most perfect time. Post it on Facebook, pin it on Pinterest. Share the smile—it's contagious.

Day 6: Think of three people you know who bring a smile to your face. Write them a note, an e-mail, a text, or give them a call and tell them that they are a smile generator for you!

Day 7: Reflect on and write your response to the following questions:

- What did you learn about smiling this week?
- How do you feel when you smile?
- How can you remember to make smiles part of your daily life?

> What sunshine is to flowers, smiles are to humanity. These are but trifles, to be sure; but, scattered along life's pathway, the good they do is inconceivable.
>
> —JOSEPH ADDISON

WEEK 5

Use the Creative Power of Your Word

> The word is not just a sound or a written symbol. The word is a force; it is the power you have to express and communicate, to think, and thereby to create the events of your life.
>
> —DON MIGUEL RUIZ

Honoring and understanding the creative power of your word, what you say and what you think, is the foundation for the experience you create each and every day. The first words of the Bible are, "In the Beginning was the word, and the word was with God, and the word was God." In the bestselling book *The Four Agreements,* don Miguel Ruiz describes four agreements to live by to experience heaven on earth. The first agreement is to be impeccable with your word.

At first I thought this simply meant that if I say I will meet you at five o'clock, then I make sure to keep that agreement. If for some reason it were not possible for me to keep the agreement, I would do my best to let you know. As I consciously applied this agreement in my daily life, I came to understand that while this is an important application of the agreement, the deeper meaning of being impeccable with your word is to think and say loving and accepting words about ourselves, others, and the circumstances of our lives. This is a challenge, since most of the time we are asleep to the words we say and entranced by the repeating tape of self-talk that runs in our mind.

For example, have you ever made a mistake and said, "I am so stupid," or "I never do anything right" or "I am such an idiot"? As you read this, you might be thinking, "Yeah, I've said those things; what's the big deal?" The big deal is this: What you believe is the experience you create. Keep in mind that beliefs are simply habitual thoughts charged with emotional energy that you think are truth.

Your thoughts create your reality. Your thoughts, conscious or unconscious, are the operating system of the life you create and live. If you want to see what you are thinking, look at the life you are living: it is the external expression of your thoughts.

Sit in silence each day and listen to your thoughts. When you notice self-sabotaging and judgmental thoughts, acknowledge yourself for noticing, and use your imagination to *make up* impeccable new thoughts. Start with five minutes per day and gradually extend the length of time (two minutes every hour, ten minutes twice a day, twenty minutes in one sitting—experiment).

Are you experiencing peace and happiness? If you are, consciously continue with the kind of thoughts you are having. If you are not, wake up to what you think and what you say. Think thoughts and say words that reflect a wholehearted life—beginning *now*.

How to Do It

Day 1: Make a list of statements you can say to yourself about yourself that are kind, respectful, and loving. Some examples are:

- I have a great sense of humor.
- I am loving.
- I am a great friend.
- I am reliable.
- I am a great cook.
- I am living a wholehearted life.
- I am a mighty expression of love.

Choose one of your statements each day and, first thing in the morning and before bed at night, say it, declare it, affirm it aloud while looking at yourself in a mirror. You might also write the statement on a sticky note or on your screen saver and send a reminder alert to repeat the words every hour.

Day 2: Make a list of the words you think and say about yourself that are abusive and judgmental. When you hear yourself thinking or saying these thoughts and words, have a new thought that reflects a loving relationship with yourself.

To fully live a wholehearted life, it is crucial that you not judge and criticize yourself, as this is a form of self-abuse. As soon as you notice abusive thoughts and words, acknowledge yourself for being awake and aware and have a new thought. With this increased awareness, you can make conscious choices about what you think and say, which will directly influence your experience.

Day 3: Use your feelings as your personal guidance system. When you are feeling loving, happy, peaceful, and inspired, notice the thoughts you are thinking; when you are feeling angry, unhappy, sad, frustrated, alone, or afraid, notice what you are believing at the moment. Remember that it is not bad that you are having these feelings; it is simply an indicator of the thoughts and beliefs you are experiencing. You have the power to change your thoughts and thereby change your point of view and your experience.

Day 4: Be direct. Say "I'd like to go to the movies, would you like to join me?" rather than "What do you want to do?" You can know exactly what you want when you get quiet and focused enough to listen rather than hiding what you want in questions and vague statements.

Day 5: Keep your word and honor your agreements. Notice the agreements you make with yourself and follow through with them; listen to the commitments you make with others and keep them. When you have to make changes in these agreements, choose words that reflect your integrity.

Two months ago I told someone that I planned to attend a course he was teaching. In the intervening weeks, I changed my work schedule and was no longer planning to attend his course. I left him a phone message. As I was beginning to write this chapter he called and asked me about the course. I told him, "It didn't work for me to take the course right now." He suggested that if this timing didn't work, he could be flexible with the schedule. I continued to say that it didn't work for me, and finally he asked, "Is it that you prefer not to take my class now or is it that the schedule doesn't work for you?" As I heard his question I knew that the truth was I preferred not to take the course now. I thanked him for his coaching. Impeccability involves being clear about what is true for me and saying what I mean!

Day 6: Put reminders around your home and workplace to honor the creative power of your word. For example:

- Thoughts are real things.
- I honor the creative power of my word.
- Eliminate gossip.
- Think love.
- Speak love.
- My experience begins with my word.

Day 7: Reflect on and write your response to the following questions:

- What did you notice this week when you focused on the words you think and say?
- What are your challenges in being conscious of your thoughts and words?
- What helps you to remember to use the creative power of your words to nourish your whole-hearted life?

WEEK 6

Commit First

> Our commitments are that which we orbit around. They are our sun, and they feed us the ability to organize our lives around that which is meaningful to us.
>
> — KATHERINE WOODWARD THOMAS

Living a wholehearted life is a conscious choice that begins with a commitment—a commitment that blossoms when it is nourished every day in your thoughts, words and actions. Often you wait to make a commitment until you are certain that all the *i*'s are dotted and all the *t*'s are crossed and that your desired result is guaranteed. You hesitate in committing too soon, filled with fearful thoughts: *What if this doesn't work out? What if I can't do this?*

Have you ever noticed that fear and anxiety often go into overdrive when you are faced with taking a stand and making a commitment? This can occur independently of the magnitude of the specific choice being made—getting married, ending a relationship, becoming a parent, running for a political office, leaving your successful career to start your own business, going off on a travel adventure, or making a New Year's resolution to be organized, eat organic food, or meditate regularly.

All too often, when consumed by fear, you give up on your dream and allow your commitment to fear to take over. This prevents you from truly committing to your *Heartsong*.

Yet, the reality of the creative process requires that you commit first. It is your commitment to your *Dream*, the song of your heart that ultimately allows you to face your fears and make choices that cultivate wholehearted living.

The words of W. H. Murray in *The Scottish Himalayan Expedition* (1951) beautifully describe the power of committing first:

> *Until one is committed, there is hesitancy, the chance to draw back, always ineffectiveness. Concerning all acts of initiative (and creation), there is one elementary truth the ignorance of which kills countless ideas and splendid plans: that the moment one definitely commits oneself, then providence moves too. A whole stream of events issue from the decision, raising in one's favor all manner of unforeseen incidents, meetings, and material assistance, which no man could have dreamt would have come his way. I learned a deep respect for one of Goethe's*

couplets: *"Whatever you can do, or dream you can, begin it. Boldness has genius, power, and magic in it!"*

How to Do It

Day 1: With Murray's words in mind, write your response to this question: *Who would I be and what would I be doing if I knew success was guaranteed?*

Day 2: Make a list of the commitments you are hesitant to make and identify what is stopping you from making them. A simple model to explore the thoughts that challenge your willingness to make a commitment is to complete the following statement:

When I am feeling _____ (write both the emotional name of your feelings and the physical sensations you feel), *I am believing* _____ (write the thoughts and beliefs—about yourself, others and life—that are generating your feelings).

For example: *When I am feeling scared about starting a new relationship and I feel a heaviness in my heart, I am believing that there is something wrong with me that I am still single; I am believing that the men I am interested in are not interested in me; I am believing that a loving relationship with a man has always been a struggle for me.*

It may take you more than one day to identify your feelings and thoughts. Once you are clear about the thoughts that are igniting your feelings:

- Acknowledge your willingness to uncover the thoughts that are at odds with the commitment you would like to make.

- Ask yourself, *Do these thoughts support my wholehearted life?*
- Make up new thoughts that are aligned with your commitment. While you may not have faith in them immediately, you are now aware of the programming that sabotages you as well as the new programming that is aligned with your desires.

Day 3: With your responses to the exercises from Day 1 and Day 2, write down the five most important items you commit to focusing your attention and actions on. Write them in the present tense, as though you are living them today.

Here are the five commitments I made while writing this chapter and doing the daily exercises. I am focusing my attention on and consciously making choices in favor of living into these dreams:

- I am happily married, and we are living in our dream house open to family and friends.
- I am healthy in body mind spirit.
- My books, home-study programs, coaching, and mentoring are changing lives.
- I easily experience continuous financial prosperity—I always have enough to share and enough to spare.
- My award-winning documentary about focusing on the gifts of the elders inspires others and transforms the role of elders.

Day 4: Share your commitments with at least one person who is a support buddy and vision keeper. Declare your commitments, reading them passionately and purposefully, with Murray's words in mind: "*...the moment one definitely commits oneself, then providence moves too. A whole stream of events issue from the decision, raising in one's favor all manner of unforeseen incidents, meetings, and material assistance, which no man could have dreamt would have come his way.*"

Day 5: Take one action today that reflects at least one of your commitments. The action I commit to taking today is: _____ (Write the action in the past tense and notice how this simple mind game ignites a *can-do* attitude.)

Day 6: Make a promise to yourself that for the next thirty days you will write (in a journal, notebook, or on your computer) your five commitments. You may find that as you write them daily they become more refined and clearer to you, or may change completely. As you write each one, allow yourself to feel—to embody—the fulfillment of each commitment.

Day 7: Reflect on and write your responses to the following questions:

- What did you learn about making commitments this week?
- What was most challenging to you about making commitments?
- What was most surprising to you?

WEEK 7

Smell the Flowers

I was not looking now at an unusual flower arrangement.

I was seeing what Adam had seen on the morning of his creation—

the miracle, moment by moment, of naked existence.

—ALDOUS HUXLEY

Smelling the flowers is a reminder to see the beauty and magnificence of Life. Springtime, the time of rebirth and new life, is the perfect time to literally and figuratively smell the flowers. Crocuses are in bloom, daffodils (maybe their name is really *daffy-dils*) are smiling, trees are wearing their Easter outfits of new buds, and Passover celebrates freedom from bondage. Nature is freely blooming.

Whatever circumstance you are experiencing in your life, stop and smell the flowers, whatever the season might be. Use all your senses—see the magic of rebirth and new life in your world, taste the deliciousness of life, touch and feel the sensations of life through your skin, delight in the glorious aromas in your world. Your senses let you know you are alive; flowers are mirrors of the cycles of life. Allow your blossoms to open, allow yourself to experience the beauty and mystery of life.

How to Do It

Day 1: Stop and smell the flowers as you walk to work, pass a flower shop, or anywhere you notice flowers as you go through your day. Choose an image of flowers for your screen saver.

Day 2: Buy yourself some flowers—a single flower or a bouquet is fine —and get to know that flower. Meditate on it, greet it, ask it questions and listen to its answers. Keep its dried petals as a reminder of the natural cycles of life, the creative process of all things: germination, birth, life, death—and then it continues over and over and over again.

Day 3: Plant some seeds, in a garden or a pot, and nourish them with your thoughts and care. As a child I watched my mom take the seeds from grapefruits and put them in a pot of soil on the windowsill. Time passed, and soon she had a beautiful plant. She continued to add seeds to the pot for as long as there was space. Last night I added three grapefruit seeds to my foot-tall grapefruit tree. Thanks, Mom, for teaching me to love life and to plant seeds so they may grow, reminding me of the cycles of life.

Day 4: Send flowers to a loved one. Send flowers to a hospital or nursing home. Give your boss, coworkers, doorman, or mail carrier a flower.

Day 5: Visit a garden. Look through gardening books and see the variety of flowers in the world.

Day 6: Identify the precious flowers in your life—family members, friends, coworkers, and members of your community—and tell them how their beauty enriches your life.

Day 7: In your journal, draw, paint, make a collage, or write a song, poem, or essay about what you learned this week, smelling the flowers. Pretend you are a flower and bloom.

> Some people are always grumbling because roses have thorns. I am grateful that thorns have roses.
>
> —ALPHONSE KARR
>
> ...and then the day came when the risk to remain tight in a bud was more painful than the risk it took to blossom.
>
> —ANAÏS NIN
>
> Be like the flower, turn your faces to the sun.
>
> —KAHLIL GIBRAN

WEEK 8

Take a New Path

Whenever I draw a circle, I immediately want to step
out of it.

—R. BUCKMINSTER FULLER

Taking a new path opens doors of possibility and
awakens you more fully to the present moment. Human
beings follow the path of least resistance. This idea in
action is seen in the habitual patterns we follow in the
course of our daily life. For example: Your alarm clock
goes off. As you reach for the snooze button, with your
eyes closed, you think, "Just five more minutes." You roll
over, and the next thing you know, your alarm clock is
beeping again. You get out of bed; your eyes are partially
open as you go into the bathroom, pee, brush your teeth,
turn on the shower, step inside, and sigh as you feel the
water against your body. This is a routine, a well-trod

path. Habits provide a structure that enables you to easily perform routine tasks. The danger is, you often continue with unconscious default patterns because you are used to them, when they are no longer effective and satisfying.

In addition to habits in your actions, you have habitual patterns of thoughts and words. You do them on automatic. The point of taking a new path is to be awake to your patterns and create new brain pathways in your thoughts, words, and actions when the old ones no longer contribute to living life to the fullest.

How the Brain Works
(Adapted from *The Inspired Life*)

A mind once stretched by a new idea, never regains its original dimension.
— OLIVER WENDELL HOLMES, JR.

Since living a wholehearted life has its roots in your mind, it is necessary to understand how your mind works and how new brain pathways are created—how upgraded software of the mind is installed.

Your mind is constantly changing. Every time you have a new thought, a new neural pathway is formed in your brain—a new train of thought. To live life to the fullest, alive and awake with passion and purpose, your mind must cultivate empowering thoughts through your beliefs, assumptions, agreements, words, feelings, choices, and actions.

When you learn something new or think a new

thought, this new brain pathway or connection is initially weak. The more frequently you focus on and act on the new thought, the stronger the brain pathway becomes.

Here's how it works: The brain is made up of cells called neurons. These cells have nerve endings called synapses and dendrites. Nerve endings release chemical and electrical stimuli to communicate with each other. This communication forms neural pathways in the brain and is the basis for how the brain works. For every thought you have, there is a corresponding communication between the neurons in your brain.

When you initially learn something, the pathway is weak. Neural pathways that are habitually used (consciously or unconsciously) are the "path well traveled." It is easy for your mind to follow these pathways, these routes, and they become your dominant and automatic thoughts and beliefs.

Think about when you first learned to ride a bike. You had to consciously pay attention to staying balanced, keeping your eyes on the road, holding onto the handlebars, and steering in your desired direction. Then, the more you practiced, the stronger your bicycle-riding brain pathways became.

Eventually you were able to get on your bike and ride without thinking. You were operating on automatic. A strong brain pathway had been created, as though a new brain software application had been uploaded and was seamlessly operating in your mind.

This week, you will practice taking a new path, which will require you to be awake and alert.

How to Do It

Day 1: Take a new path to the places you go. Drive down a different road on your way to work. Take a bus instead of the car, or park your car a few blocks from where you are going and walk the rest of the way. Use the stairs at work instead of the elevator. Pick the kids up from school today rather than having them take the school bus. Play with this. Be creative.

Day 2: Change the way you normally do things. If you always brush your teeth before you shower, today take your toothbrush into the shower with you and brush your teeth in the shower. If you usually automatically turn on the TV when you are fixing breakfast, today, leave it off, and focus your attention on consciously preparing and eating your breakfast. Are birds singing, are your kids laughing, is there an argument you can hear, what does the running water sound like? Sit at a different place at your table. Experiment writing with your non-dominant hand. Sleep on the other side of the bed. Play with taking a new path.

Day 3: Do something different with what you wear. Wear that sexy underwear you've been saving. Wear your hair down if you usually wear it up. Wear a tie that makes you smile rather than the one that you always wear with your corporate uniform. Paint your fingernails with the gold glitter nail polish that made you smile when you saw it on your daughter's fingernails. Wear no makeup for the day. Play. Enjoy. Take a new path.

Day 4: Notice your thoughts today. When you become aware that your thoughts are taking you down a hellish road, have a new thought. Notice, when you put your mind to it, that you can turn lemon thoughts into refreshing lemonade.

Recently, as I was leaving a friend's house to drive home after having visited over a holiday weekend, he said to me, "Get ready for a long drive, you're going to get into a lot of holiday traffic." That wasn't the farewell idea that I wanted to be thinking as I began my long journey home. I went over to him and said, "Imagine I have an easy, smooth drive home, and that I call and let you know that traffic was light and my drive was relaxing."

Having a new thought, creating a new pathway in your thinking, is magical. Experiment. (And I did have an easy drive home. I even got on an earlier ferry!)

Day 5: Create a new path in your life that opens the door wide to peace of mind. Here are some possibilities:

- Signing up for a regular yoga class
- Beginning each day with an inspirational reading
- Enjoying the quiet of each morning in silence
- Taking a bubble bath before you go to sleep
- Scheduling a regular massage
- Writing an appreciation list of what you are grateful for before you go to sleep
- Buying a subscription to your local theater

Let your heart be your guide as you create this new path in your life.

Day 6: Do something you have been putting off or have been *afraid* to do. Get your hair colored. Buy and wear rose-colored sunglasses. Have a makeover at the makeup counter in your local department store. Get home before your lover, fill your bedroom with candles, and have a romantic dinner in bed. Audition for a play in your community theater. Join the choir. Wear a sexy outfit. Express your ideas at work. Talk to that person in the gym who you think is so attractive.

Day 7: Reflect on and write your response to the following questions:

- What did you discover?
- How can you use this idea in your daily life?
- How does taking a new path illuminate your life?

Autobiography in Five Short Chapters

by Portia Nelson

I

I walk down the street.
There is a hole in the sidewalk.
I fall in.
I am lost...I am helpless.
It isn't my fault.
It takes forever to find my way out.

II

I walk down the same street.
There is a deep hole in the sidewalk.
I pretend I don't see it.
I fall in again.
I can't believe I am in the same place.
But it isn't my fault.
It still takes a long time to get out.

III

I walk down the same street.
There is a deep hole in the sidewalk.
I see it there.
I still fall in...it's a habit.
My eyes are open.
I know where I am.
It is my fault.
I get out immediately.

IV
I walk down the same street.
There is a deep hole in the sidewalk.
I walk around it.

V
I walk down another street.

WEEK 9

Create a Daily Ritual

Religious ritual is a way of structuring time so that we, not employers, the market, or the media, are in control. Life needs its pauses, its chapter breaks, if the soul is to have space to breathe.

—JONATHAN SACKS

Living a wholehearted life requires a deep connection and alignment of body mind spirit. In Western culture—focused on *doing* rather than *being*, on the external material world rather than the internal intuitive world—we are often out of alignment. A daily ritual, a spiritual practice—which may or may not be grounded in a specific religious tradition—serves the function of aligning our body mind spirit, just as a chiropractic adjustment aligns our body.

At different times in my life I have created and followed different daily rituals. What has been consistent in all of my practices through the years has been some form of mediation and journaling. We will focus on these specific practices later in the book (see Week 16. Write Down Your Soul, page 85, and Week 19. Meditate, page 107).

You can think of a daily ritual as an exercise program for wholehearted living. Just as physical exercise has to be practiced on a regular basis to maintain a strong, toned, and flexible body, your daily spiritual practice strengthens your connection with your inner world and serves to align body mind spirit.

Reverend Diane Berke, the founder and spiritual director of One Spirit Learning Alliance, describes this beautifully:

> *The times we spend in prayer and meditation, in whatever forms are most resonant for us, are like building spiritual muscle. Through regular practice we develop qualities of strength, flexibility, endurance, and balance. We develop wisdom, faith, equanimity, kindness; we develop honesty and self-acceptance. We cultivate our ability to let go, our capacity to forgive, our capacity to be present to this moment. We learn to deeply listen, and to open ourselves to grace.*
>
> *Then, when we need those qualities and skills in our lives, they are there for us to draw upon and use. And our very presence may become a gift of healing, inspiration, and potential transformation to others.*

How to Do It

Day 1: Create your own daily ritual, keeping in mind the following components so your ritual will activate all of your senses:

1. Preparation—Identify a specific sacred space in your home. This may be a particular room or a special chair that embraces you like a loving hug. One of my coaching clients would go into the bathroom with a pillow and candle since it was the only room in the house where her family respected her privacy! These days, sitting on my bed with comfortable pillows supporting my back is my morning and evening sacred space. You might burn sage to smudge, cleanse, and purify the space each day, but this is not necessary—particularly if it might activate a smoke detector!

2. Activate Your Senses—Engaging your senses allows your whole being to be activated during your ritual. As part of your preparation, you may use a candle, scented oil, incense, or a fragrant flower to ignite your sense of smell; have some fruit or other food to represent the nourishment you gain from following your passions; wear a scarf, shawl or other piece of clothing that has special meaning for you—allow your sense of touch to be switched on.

3. Sequence—Remember, what is most important is that you create a ritual that is truly your own. While the details may evolve over time, or be a bit different when you are at home and when you are away, the consistency of following a particular sequence strengthens the potency of the ritual. The following is a structure that I currently use:

In the morning:
- Light two candles
- Put on my Prayer Shawl
- Randomly open a book of poetry and read a poem aloud
- Meditate for twenty minutes (this is my preferred amount of time—if you are new to mediation, you may choose to begin with five minutes).
- Write my five commitments in my journal, along with any additional ideas that were sparked during my meditation. This may include actions to take, which I write in the past tense as though they are already accomplished!
- Write one thing I am grateful for
- Write one thing I appreciate about myself or others

Before I go to sleep:
- Write three accomplishments in support of my commitments
- List five things I am grateful for—including at least one item I have never before expressed gratitude for
- List five things I appreciate—including at least one quality or action I appreciate about myself

Day 2–Day 6: Do your daily ritual.

Day 7: Do your daily ritual, then reflect on and write your response to the following questions:

- How did your daily ritual impact your day?
- What did you learn about yourself by doing this ritual?
- Are you ready to commit to a daily ritual for the next week, twenty-one days, month? Make the commitment.

WEEK 10

Sing

It is the best of all trades, to make songs, and the second best to sing them.

—HILAIRE BELLOC

Singing is an enjoyable way to change your mood and experience the present moment more fully. Singing can lift your spirit, and often the songs that pop into your mind automatically have a message for you in the moment. Chanting, which is part of a regular Hindu spiritual practice, is used as a meditation to calm your mind and transform your experience. On occasions when I have chanted in a group for an hour, I have noticed that at some point I stop singing the chant and the chant starts singing me. My experience of myself changes, and I am sound and breath and the experience of the words themselves. It is both a relaxing and an energizing experience.

The power of singing has less to do with how good your voice is and more to do with your openness to allow the song to lift you and carry you on its wings. This week experiment with singing and create a personal song library that you can go to and use as a source of comfort, joy, peace, inspiration, and vitality.

How to Do It

Day 1: Sing. Sing in the shower, sing while you're cooking, sing while you're driving to and from your errands or work. Make up songs to sing to your pets. Sing.

Day 2: Chant for thirty to sixty minutes. Download a chant, or find one at your local library or music store. Don't worry about pronouncing each word perfectly; allow the song to lead you. If you notice your mind commenting and judging, simply focus your attention back on the sounds moving through you.

One month when I was practicing chanting for thirty minutes each day, I was unable to stay focused on any particular chant. I noticed that a round from my child-hood, "Row, Row, Row Your Boat," kept going through my mind, so I used that when I chanted. Over and over and over again I repeated the words and they carried me *gently down the stream*. I realized that within this children's song, words that I had sung hundreds of times automatically without really listening, was wisdom for living a wholehearted life!

Day 3: Listen to and sing along with a kind of song that is new to you. If opera is something that is new to you, listen to great opera and allow the sounds to touch you. Don't be concerned with whether or not you understand the words—allow the sound to speak to your heart.

Day 4: Go to a karaoke club and sing. Again, this isn't about having the best voice. This is about playing through song.

Day 5: Put together a song library—it's so easy these days given the various websites that allow you to create your own stations. Songs to calm you when you need calming, songs to inspire you, sing-alongs to sing when you're in the car with your family, songs to cook by, songs to clean by, sing-along songs for when friends stop by. Remember those camp songs that you sang so many years ago, imprinted on your memory, sung around the campfire, sung when you were doing chores, all of which created a sense of camaraderie and connection. My guess is that if you simply took a deep breath, a camp song would pop into your mind. Sing it!

Day 6: If singing with a group or choir is something you have always wanted to do, do it! Join a choir, try out for your community theatre musical, take some voice lessons. Stop waiting to sing until tomorrow and do it today. If this is not something that speaks to you, then sing along with music today—in the shower, while in your car, or around the dinner table.

My mother loved to sing. When we went to the movies or the theater or watched a musical on TV, she would sing and hum along. When we were in public I was embarrassed by her singing; I would lean over toward her and in an annoyed voice say, "Shush, Mom." She would be quiet for a moment and then once again she would be captured by the song. When she was in her seventies she joined a choir and sang in nursing homes each week. Years later, when I spoke with her about this, she told me that she had loved singing and had wanted to be in a choir for years. I felt so proud and inspired by my mom, and learned an important lesson: It is never too late to step into our dreams.

Day 7: Write a song that describes the power of singing in your life and what you have learned about the power of song to allow love to flow in and out of your heart.

> When I wished to sing of love, it turned to sorrow. And when I wished to sing of sorrow, it was transformed for me into love.
>
> —SCHUBERT

WEEK 11

Live Your Dreams

Go confidently in the direction of your dreams! Live the
life you've imagined.

—HENRY DAVID THOREAU

Living your dreams is what a wholehearted life is all
about. Your dreams are your Heartsong. They are the
passion and the calling that is alive in you, an expression
of the gifts and talents you were born to bring to life,
just as a caterpillar carries within itself the potential to
be a butterfly.

Unfortunately, many of us are living our nightmare,
or waiting until tomorrow to live our dreams, or trying
to convince ourselves that our dreams are just that,
dreams, and not something real and possible in our lives.
Yet it is through wholeheartedly living our dreams that
we open doors and windows to a satisfying, fulfilling,

and joyous life. It is through living our dreams that we truly honor and value our life as a precious present.

Everything that exists in the world begins as a dream, an idea, a vision, a thought, whether it is a paperclip or a relationship, love or fear. Everything is created twice, first as a dream and then in our three-dimensional reality. We are dreamers, and when we dream with our heart, married to our thoughts and action, magic happens.

You have probably had experiences in your life where in a spurt of inspiration an idea, a dream, enters your consciousness fully formed. A vision of a new job, a relationship, a solution to a problem, or a new path to take. You feel a powerful surge of loving energy move through you as this desire, your Heartsong, captures your attention. In the moment, you decide to follow your dream.

Then life happens and you begin to doubt the possibility of your dream. If you use these times of doubt and uncertainty as springboards to recommit to your dream, as time goes by, all sorts of support will unfold. You will get the money to enroll in school; you will get the job you love; you will find venture capital for your new invention; you will create a deep, loving relationship in your life. If, on the other hand, you allow the voice of fear to be the narrator of your dream, you will decide that your Heartsong, though a nice idea, is simply not going to happen. And with that decision, you stop breathing life into your dream.

Since we are dreamers anyway, and we create our experience through an alchemical process that combines our thoughts, beliefs, faith, and energy (our *e-motion*— energy in motion), we might as well dream the dreams and live the life that we truly desire. This week, take steps to live your dreams, and when blocks and obstacles present themselves, use them simply as opportunities to strengthen your commitment to your dream. And make sure that you do not dwell on your current circumstances and thereby give them the upper hand. If you want a loving relationship, but you are single and haven't had a date in years, keep your attention on your dream, as if it is alive in the moment; if you feel trapped in your current job, dependent on your weekly paycheck and benefits, and your dream is to start your own business, don't get lost in the drama and hopelessness you feel in your current conditions. Instead, put your energy into dreaming your new business: see it, taste it, touch it, feel it, talk about it as if it exists right now, and then live into your dream.

How to Do It

Day 1: Articulate your dream. Imagine that it is one year from today and you are living your dream. Close your eyes and dream your life using the full resources of your imagination:

- Where are you living?
- Who are you living with?
- What kind of work are you doing?
- What do you feel?
- How is your health?
- How are your finances?
- How do you spend your day?
- How do you look?

Be as specific as you can. Allow your dream to enter your consciousness. If unknown people or places appear in your dream, simply allow yourself to become familiar with them.

When you have a clear sense of your dream filling your being, open your eyes and write a description of your dream in the present tense. On the top of the page, write the date, one year from today, and begin your first sentence with: *I am...*

(To be inspired by stories of people who are living their life filled with passion and purpose, listen to my weekly On Purpose Radio Show at http://bit.ly/Purpose-Podcast.)

Day 2: Twice a day, read and visualize your Day 1 dream. Make adjustments based on new ideas and information. Remember, this is a fluid and evolving process. The title of this book changed many times in the process of writing it! Close your eyes and step into your dream. Experience it, enjoy it, fill in the details, feel a sense of excitement and satisfaction fill your being as a smile lights up your face. When you have fully dreamed your dream—this may take as little as thirty seconds or as long as twenty minutes—ask your still small voice, "What is my next step in living my dream?" Listen to the answer and then *do it*. It is important that you open to the loving wisdom of the universe, that still small voice, for your next step, rather than doing what you think you *should* do. Sometimes your next step is simply to enjoy the day!

Day 3: Make a Bucket List. Write one hundred dreams and desires you have that you would like to experience during your life. Write down whatever enters your consciousness. Once you have your list written, read it and put a check mark next to those dreams you are ready to take action on today. For the items without a check mark, write them again on a list entitled *For the Universe to Provide*. As you write each dream on this list, know that it is now in the loving hands of the universe. Have faith that the universe is at work; your only job is to be available to the instructions of the still small voice within and to allow your dream to take form in your life. It is okay if you put all one hundred items on this list. Your job is to express your dream. The universe illuminates the path, and you allow your dream as long as you are vibrationally aligned and open to receiving—believing you deserve it and trusting that your prayers are answered at the perfect time.

Day 4: Create a collage of your dream. As you do this, feel your dream alive in your being. Feel the excitement in your body. Make sure to include an image of yourself in your collage.

Day 5: Create a dream support buddy relationship. Share your dream with one person who has total faith in your ability to live your dreams. Ask that person to keep you focused when and if your faith in your dreams, your faith in the universe, or your faith in God wavers.

Day 6: Be your dream. Today, make everything you think, say and do a reflection of you living your dream. If doubt presents itself, simply have a new thought in the next moment. What would you think, say, feel, do if:

- ...you had a great golf score?
- ...you had beautiful nails?
- ...your marriage was delightful?

- ...you were in a loving relationship?
- ...you had financial prosperity?
- ...you experienced well-being?
- ...you were an artist?
- ...you had your own successful business?
- ...you were living your dreams?

Day 7: Reflect and write your response to the following questions:

- What did you notice when you consciously focused on living your dreams?
- Do you hold back from dreaming your dreams because you are afraid you won't get them, or because you are afraid you will get them?
- Do you worry that you have to make your dreams happen, or do you have faith in your co-creative partnership with the universe?

> I do not know how to distinguish between our waking life and a dream. Are we not always living the life that we imagine we are?
>
> —THOREAU

WEEK 12
Eliminate Gossip

> Gossip is black magic at its very worst because it is pure poison. We learned how to gossip by agreement. When we were children, we heard the adults around us gossiping all the time, openly giving their opinions about other people. They even had opinions about people they didn't know. Emotional poison was transferred along with the opinions, and we learned this as the normal way to communicate.
>
> —DON MIGUEL RUIZ

Eliminating gossip is a powerful way to honor the creative power of your word. Gossip is a form of judgment and abuse, whether about yourself or others. While the intent is not always malicious, the telling and retelling of a story charged with emotional fuel tends to reinforce drama. Remember, your words have creative power: What you think and say, charged with emotional energy (energy in motion), is what you create in your experience.

Gossip is like casting a spell, feeding a story of woe, and reinforcing the exact behavior that annoys you to begin with. If you feel yourself eager to spread the news about so-and-so, or if you are in search of someone to tell about the continuing drama of your life, just don't do it! At first, this might feel uncomfortable, since, in general, so much of our communication is about our opinions of others or about some continuing saga in our own lives.

Some of us (like me), who have experienced talk therapy, have become so adept at *sharing* our story that when we eliminate gossip, we initially are at a loss about what to say to others. Keep in mind that silence is okay, even though you may not be used to it. Commenting on the present moment, the sound of the wind, the fragrance of honeysuckle in the air, the magnificence of a majestic sunset, or the taste of the food you are eating are all acceptable ways to make conversation.

Eliminate gossip this week, and if you find yourself eager to get into the muck and mire of a juicy story, with many twists and turns in the plot, take a deep breath and choose, in the moment, to eliminate gossip.

How to Do It

Day 1: Think before you speak. If it's gossip, don't say it. If you're not sure whether or not it is gossip, don't say it.

Day 2: Notice when you do gossip and stop, or change the conversation.

Day 3: When you are with others who are gossiping, practice saying, "I'd prefer not gossiping about _____" or "Rather than gossiping about _____, let's talk about what's working in our lives" or "I'm practicing not gossiping and fueling the drama in my life.

Would you help me by changing the subject?" Or simply change the subject. (*Yum, the sauce on this pasta is delicious. Jamie, that's a great color of nail polish. I'd love your help planning my next vacation, Pat, what's your favorite vacation place?* And that old standby, the weather, is always something you can comment on!)

Day 4: Share good news about what is going on in your life.

Day 5: Notice how often the conversations you are involved in are based on gossip. The more you become aware of this, the more you can change the course of a conversation midstream or simply remove yourself from it. Make sure you do not go on a crusade and judge others. Simply practice eliminating gossip and notice how that impacts those around you.

Day 6: Share with five people what you have learned about yourself and eliminating gossip this week.

Day 7: Reflect on and write your response to the following questions:

- What did you learn about yourself?
- What made it hard to eliminate gossip; what made it easy?
- How do you plan to continue eliminating gossip in your life?

The Monk and the Peasant

by Margaret E. Bruner

A peasant once unthinkingly spread tales about a friend.
But later found the rumors false and hoped to make amend.
He sought the counsel of a monk, a man esteemed and wise,
Who heard the peasant's story through and felt he must advise.
The kind monk said: "If you would have a mind again at peace,
I have a plan whereby you may from trouble find release.
Go fill a bag with chicken down and to each dooryard go
And lay one fluffy feather where the streams of gossip show."
The peasant did as he was told and to the monk returned,
Elated that his penance was a thing so quickly earned.
"Not yet," the old monk sternly said, "Take up your bag once more
And gather up the feathers that you placed at every door."
The peasant, eager to atone, went hastening to obey,
No feathers met his sight, the wind had blown them all away.

WEEK 13

Live Life as a Thank-You

If the only prayer you ever say in your life is thank you,
it will be enough.

— MEISTER ECKHART

Living life as a thank-you is a clear expression of gratitude for what we have attracted into our lives and an
appreciation of the co-creative process. People seem to
have more practice noticing what isn't working and what
is lacking in their lives than they do noticing the infinite
possibilities in their world. This is a learned habit. Practicing gratitude and appreciation creates a new habit
pattern in your thoughts and behaviors, allowing you
to experience the world through a new point of view.
Strengthening your perception of gratitude requires
repetition. It begins with your intent to nurture this
viewpoint and notice where you consciously put your

attention. If you notice that your attention is lacking, acknowledge yourself for noticing and then focus your attention on what is abundant in your life, what you are grateful for. If you notice that your consciousness is focused on gratitude, give yourself a pat on the back to reinforce the strengthening of an attitude of gratitude in your life.

How to Do It

Day 1: When you wake up in the morning, express your gratitude for the gift of the new day, and before you go to sleep at night, express your appreciation for the day you've lived. For many years, I ended my day by saying, "Thank you for another day of Loving."

Day 2: Once an hour, stop what you are doing and focus on what you are grateful for.

Day 3: Before you go to sleep, write down five things you are grateful for on this day (*I am grateful for my health, I am grateful for my family, I am grateful that I flossed my teeth, I am grateful for my eyesight, I am grateful for the sun rising this morning, I am grateful that I meditated for twenty minutes, I am grateful that I remembered to be grateful!* and so forth). This is a powerful daily practice. Do it every day for a month and notice the shift in perception you experience having strengthened your muscle of appreciation. Continue doing it every day.

Day 4: Find inspiring quotes about gratitude and put them on your refrigerator. Enter them as reminders in your smartphone, on your calendar, and on your screen saver. When you notice them, stop for a moment and express your gratitude for the life you have and the people in it.

Day 5: Express your gratitude throughout the day by saying "Thank you." Set a challenge for yourself: *Today I am saying "Thank you" fifty times, one hundred times, or even more!* Remember to play with this. You may say "Thank you" to the person driving slowly in the car in front of you, for giving you an opportunity to practice patience! See if you can find at least one thing to be thankful for in every situation you are in today.

Day 6: Begin a daily practice of identifying one thing each day for which you have never before expressed your appreciation. For instance:

- I am grateful my toenails grow.
- I am grateful for the wrinkly lines on my fingers that make it easy for me to bend them.
- I am grateful for the parents of the person at the checkout counter of the supermarket who smiled at me today while checking out my groceries.
- I'm grateful for the stylus that makes my touch screen so easy to use.

Day 7: Reflect on and write your response to the following questions:

- How did focusing on what you are grateful for impact your life?
- How can you incorporate being grateful into your daily life? Do it.

Both abundance and lack exist simultaneously in our lives, as parallel realities. It is always our conscious choice which secret garden we will tend. When we choose not to focus on what is missing from our lives but are grateful for the abundance that's present—love, health, family, friends, work, the joys of nature and personal pursuits that bring us pleasure—the wasteland of illusion falls away and we experience Heaven on Earth.

—SARAH BAN BREATHNACH,
FROM *SIMPLE ABUNDANCE*

We have all experienced being around people who find beauty at every turn of the road. They are really and truly grateful for each and every encounter—the smile on a stranger's face, the kindness of a barista. When we are with those people, it sets our vibrations higher; it makes us aware that we are responsible for attracting all those things that will make our lives complete.

—NINA LESOWITZ AND
MARY BETH SAMMONS,
FROM *LIVING LIFE AS A THANK YOU*

WEEK 14
Write Your Obituary

Obituary: a notice of a person's death with a short biographical account.

—MERRIAM-WEBSTER'S
COLLEGIATE DICTIONARY

Let me take a moment to acknowledge that many people have told me, over the years, that the thought of writing their obituary makes them uncomfortable or gives them the creeps. If that is the case for you, take a deep breath and be aware that we don't acknowledge that death is a part of life. It is often too easy to think we have forever to live our dreams, yet all that we are assured of is right now, the precious present moment.

If you are more comfortable with the idea of writing a eulogy, then write a eulogy. If both *obituary* and *eulogy* are words that make you uncomfortable, think about what beloved family and friends would say about your life as they gather with you for your 100th birthday celebration.

Writing your obituary is a powerful way to focus on what is important to you in your life. It gives you an opportunity to think about and articulate how you want the life you have lived to be described. It highlights your intrinsic values and can remind you of your priorities and heart's desires. It is a life-giving exercise, focusing your imagination, intentions, and actions on your vision of your life. When you do this exercise this week, don't limit yourself by what you think is possible. Open your heart and allow your imagination to do what it does best: Imagine and listen to the still small voice within that answers when you ask, "What do I want said about my life when I die?" And remember, the Angel of Death is always present, so it is a good idea to live today the life you desire to live. I have learned that in the presence of the Angel of Death, Love is present when we allow ourselves to be wholeheartedly awake.

How to Do It

Day 1: Still your mind:

- Sit comfortably.
- Close your eyes.
- Focus on your breath.
- Follow the path of your breath as it enters your body through your nose, circulates throughout your body, and leaves your body through your mouth. Do this for five inhalations and exhalations. Ask yourself the question, "What do I want said about the life I've lived?" Listen to the answer and write it down.

Day 2: Make a list of what is important to you: the people in your life, the roles you play, the activities you do. From this list, identify what truly makes your heart sing. Are these the things you currently focus on? If yes, continue. If no, choose one item on your list and begin it today.

Day 3: Jot down phrases for your headstone—for example, "She lived well," "He lived a wholehearted life," "She was the world's greatest lover"—and then elaborate on what that phrase actually means to you. Allow your imagination to flow as you explain and build on the phrase.

Day 4: Make a collage that represents the kind of life you choose to live. Allow your heart and your imagination to be your guide. As you create your collage, ask yourself the question, "Who would I be and what would I be doing if I knew success was guaranteed?" Listen to the answer and allow your collage to represent your heart's desire. Make sure to include a photograph of yourself in your collage.

Day 5: Live today as though it was your last day on earth. Make each moment count. One of my most powerful and inspiring memories of September 11 is hearing about the cell phone calls from people who were facing death to their loved ones expressing their love. This is a powerful illustration that in the presence of the Angel of Death, what is truly important—expressing our love—takes a leading role in our lives. Express your love today.

Day 6: Write your obituary and put it somewhere where you will read it daily. This is the vision of the life you choose to create. Take time each day and check to see if the way you are living reflects the life you desire to live. If it does, allow yourself to feel energized, knowing that the life you are living is aligned with the life you desire to live. If the life you are living and the life you desire to live are at odds with one another, start making changes. Begin in your imagination, seeing the life you desire, and then begin to see it and take action in your daily life, allowing your heart's desire to unfold, having faith that it is.

Day 7: Reflect on and write your response to the following questions:

- What did you discover by focusing on your life?
- How can you use this information to live whole-heartedly each and every day?

The Power of an Obituary

Many years ago I heard a story about Alfred B. Nobel, whose directions in his will resulted in the creation of the Nobel Peace Prize. Alfred's family was in the explosives business. When one of his brothers died, Alfred's obituary was mistakenly published in the newspaper. He read his obituary, which highlighted his business successes in the manufacturing of dynamite. Reading his obituary was the impetus to change the direction of his life. Now, when Alfred Nobel is mentioned, we associate the name with the Nobel Peace Prize—not with explosives!

WEEK 15

Spend Time with a Friend

Each friend represents a world in us, a world possibly not born until they arrive, and it is only by this meeting that a new world is born.

—ANAÏS NIN

Spending time with a friend is a gift of love you give yourself. Friends are treasures. They giggle with us, they remind us of who we are, and they are a mirror that sheds light on our shadow and our radiance. They are a shoulder to cry on, a buddy to do things with, and a lifeline when the road gets rough. Spending time with a friend is a vital root which nourishes your well-being. This week, cultivate this treasure of life by spending time with a friend.

How to Do It

Day 1: Spend time with a friend today. Call a friend on the spur of the moment and make plans to meet for lunch, or settle in on the couch with the phone and talk with your best friend who lives in another part of the country.

Day 2: Send a card to a friend today that expresses your love and care for this special being in your life.

Day 3: Do a friendship inventory:

- Who are the friends who you can call anytime, day or night, when you need a shoulder to cry on?
- Who are the friends you can count on to confront you, the ones who remind you that you have been singing that tune for many months now, and ask how they can help you to move on?
- Who are the friends you enjoy doing things with?
- Who are the friends who tell you what they think, not simply what they think you want to hear?
- Who are the friends to share adventures with?
- Who are the friends you allow yourself to be vulnerable with, the ones you call late at night when you are feeling alone, the ones you are eager to share good news with?

After you have completed your inventory, notice what this tells you. Are there any changes you want to make? Make them!

Day 4: Make a friendship celebration date with a friend or group of friends. This is a day to celebrate your friendship. You may go out and get a manicure together, go to your favorite sporting event, eat at your favorite restaurant, or share a meal you've cooked together in one of your homes. Make sure you use some of your time together to express and acknowledge that this time is a celebration of your friendship.

Day 5: Get in touch with an old friend whom you have wondered about. Call the last phone number you have for her, send a note to his last address, do a search on Facebook for her. If none of that works, have a conversation in your mind with him. Let her know that you are thinking of her and that you'd love the opportunity to reconnect. Have faith that this communication is getting to her.

I have two childhood friends whom I sought out in my consciousness for many years. They would pop into my mind from time to time, and I felt I was putting a call out into the universe for them. In each case, a few years later they popped up, each at the most perfect time. One of them I am still in touch with. We first met when our mothers took us to the local park in our baby carriages when we were a few months old. I love this connection with someone who knew me way back when. The other friend and I stayed in touch briefly, and she shared with me her perception of me when we were teenagers. It was a powerful reminder that my perception of myself when I was a teen had been quite judgmental and abusive. She gave me a new perspective that opened the door for me to upgrade my personal history!

Day 6: Today, be your best friend. Treat yourself as though you are a treasure. See yourself through the eyes of your best friend. Be gentle, be loving, be accepting, be your own best friend.

Day 7: Reflect on and write your response to the following questions:

- What did you learn about friendship in your life?
- How do your friendships contribute to living your best life?
- Are there any changes you want to make? Make them!

> *Oh the comfort of feeling safe with a person,*
> *Of having neither to weigh thoughts nor measure words*
> *But pouring them all out, wheat and chaff together,*
> *Knowing that a faithful hand will take and sift them*
> *Keeping what is worth keeping and, with a breath of kindness...Blow the rest away.*
> —MACKIE AYRES

The greatest sweetener of human life is friendship.

—JOSEPH ADDISON

WEEK 16

Write Down Your Soul

I never know what I think about something until I read what I've written on it.

—WILLIAM. FAULKNER

Keeping a diary, writing daily pages, and journaling are powerful practices that open the door to who you are, what you are thinking, and your intuitive inner wisdom—the still, small voice within. They can guide you through the murk and mire of overwhelming emotions and drama, and illuminate the path from darkness right (write!) into the light.

Janet Conner, the author of *Writing Down Your Soul,* writes, "You could pray, or meditate, or dream, or visit a shaman, or a minister, or a hypnotherapist. With so many routes into inner consciousness, why write? Of all the ways to get in touch with God, as you understand

God...to hear the small, still voice pointing you in the right direction...why take the time to write? One reason: it works. It works amazingly well. If you want to engage in a vibrant conversation with the wisdom that dwells just a hair below your conscious awareness, write."

Journaling can be done with a question in mind, as a way to record your day, or stream-of-consciousness, by putting pen to paper and writing whatever comes to mind. Whether a regular writing practice is a new technique for you, or you have been keeping a journal since you got your first diary as a child that came with a lock and key and the word *Diary* written in gold letters, journal writing provides a direct connection between your inner and outer life—a connection that is the fertile soil of a wholehearted life.

There have been times in my life that my journal has been my best friend, accepting all I write with no judgments, and always available. After spending time writing in my journal, I feel renewed. I began writing in a diary when I was a child. My journals took up a couple of shelves on a bookcase. They were all sizes, shapes, and fabrics, handmade by artists or factory-made and mass-produced. I have drawn in them, written in them, used special pens, and been a poet in them. I have written my secret thoughts and my heart's desires. I have written about how others have been mean to me and how I have been cruel to others. I have made lists of plans. For many years when I was single I wrote in a special journal that was a call to the universe for my mate. I envisioned I would give this beautiful flowered book to him when we married. Years later, I gave it to him on our wedding night. As I write this, I'm single again and I have written another journal as a call to my mate for the next chapter of my life!

In 2002 I read through many of my journals and noticed how often I repeated dramas in which I was not enough: not pretty enough, not smart enough, not thin enough, not wealthy enough. I realized those old stories were no longer the central theme in my life. I began to think that it might be time to burn my journals. While this idea immediately captured my attention, I also felt afraid. Who would I be if I were no longer attached to this idea of myself? So I turned to my journal and wrote and wrote and wrote some more.

On March 17, 2003, I burned my journals—and they served me, yet again, as my old story transformed into ashes that I used as fertilizer in my garden to nourish new blooms as my commitment to living a wholehearted life was set on course to blossom.

Enjoy writing down your soul this week and notice the impact of writing (righting) in your life when you journal as a daily practice.

How to Do It

Day 1: If you have a journal, use it; if you don't, get one, or create a journal folder on your computer. (I admit there is something about actually writing with a pen on paper that feels just right to me. Experiment with what works best for you.) Your journal can be a special book you love seeing and touching, or simply a spiral notebook. You may use a special pen you love, or use any pen that is nearby. Journal writing is a pathway to an intimate relationship with yourself, so honor this relationship.

For ten minutes, write anything that comes to your mind, even if what comes to your mind is, *"I don't know what to write.*" Simply write for ten minutes. If you are stumped about how to start, and the blank page feels like an enemy, you can begin by writing, *"Today I am writing in my journal for ten minutes."*

Day 2: Write *from* your soul for fifteen minutes today about your heart's desire. You may notice, when you have finished writing for fifteen minutes, that there is variation in your handwriting in different parts of what you have written. I have noticed that my handwriting is very much influenced by what I am feeling. Often during one session of writing I feel many feelings that are all expressed through my handwriting. This is one reason that I prefer to write down my soul with pen on paper rather than on a computer.

Day 3: Choose a topic, issue, or question you are concerned about or have been battling with and write about it for fifteen minutes. Some possibilities are:

- Who would I be and what would I be doing if I knew success was guaranteed?
- My ideal job is:_____.
- How can I be loving with my family?
- What are the beliefs of someone who experiences financial prosperity?
- How can I experience greater well-being?
- How can I see _____ (name a challenge you are facing) through the eyes of love?
- How can I forgive _____ (yourself or someone else)?
- What are the gifts and talents that I am here to share?

Remember, if at any point while you are writing you hear your inner voice saying, "I don't know what else to write about this," write that down. Write whatever pops into your mind. This is not about creating a literary masterpiece. Writing down your soul is about you communicating with you.

Day 4: Any time during the day when you are feeling off-center, anxious, worried, or isolated, stop what you are doing as soon as you can and write what you are feeling. Allow whatever words come to mind to flow out through your pen or keyboard. Write until you are feeling all right again. This is a very potent way to acknowledge what you are feeling and to move through it. When you resist feeling what you feel, the thoughts that have generated the feelings persist and continue to directly influence your perception. When you are honest about what you are feeling and acknowledge your emotions, you are able to move through them and move on. Remember that feelings are generated by thoughts—thoughts that you may or may not be conscious of—and they are temporary when acknowledged.

Day 5: Write your personal history from the point of view of being *enough*—good enough, smart enough, handsome enough, beautiful enough, athletic enough, sexy enough, lovable enough. For some of us, this is a stretch, because the traumas and dramas of our lives have been the main themes of our personal histories. So, if you were raised in an abusive family, rather than focus on that, write about your next-door neighbor who always had a kind word for you. You now have the opportunity to free yourself from an old story that no longer serves you and to write a new one. You may be surprised, as you engage in this exercise, at the buried happy memories that pop up. Do this for at least fifteen minutes.

Day 6: Choose any topic or simply follow your stream of consciousness and write down your soul for fifteen minutes.

Day 7: Reflect and write your response to the following questions:

- What was your experience journaling?
- How did you feel after writing each day?
- If you didn't write each day, what stopped you?
- Do you prefer having a specific topic or writing stream-of-consciousness or both?
- How did writing down your soul contribute to your feeling wholehearted—connected inside and out?

> Writing crystallizes thought and thought produces action.
>
> —PAUL J. MEYER

WEEK 17

Adorn Yourself

Some people save new clothes to wear for a "special occasion."...What is today's date? This date is special. Go put on something "special"—something you have been saving. See how it feels.

—EVE ELIOT

Adorning yourself, wearing your favorite outfit and accessories, is a way of honoring and celebrating yourself. And if you want to be adored, you've got to start by adoring yourself! You may have many favorite outfits, depending on the role you are playing at a particular time. Can you imagine how you would feel if you were always wearing your favorite outfit? Sometimes it would be those worn, comfy sweatpants that you sigh into with a sense of relaxation as you feel them embrace your body. Other times it would be your special dress-up clothes; simply seeing them on a hanger in your closet puts a smile on your face, and when you wear them you feel handsome and dashing, sexy and beautiful, radiant and playful. Some of us, though, are waiting to wear our favorite outfit, just like we are waiting to use the good dishes. Are you waiting for the right occasion? Until you are the right weight? Or are you worried that you might spill something or get a stain on your favorite cashmere sweater, so you keep it neatly folded on a shelf in your closet? It catches your attention every so often, and you even take it out and try it on, but when you think about it you decide that today, now, is not the time to wear it. When the right day finally comes, you may discover that moths got to enjoy it before you did!

Wholehearted living is about actually living your life, being fully alive, engaged in this great mystery of creation. Remember, you are an artist, and your greatest creation is the life you live. One of the most powerful ways you have to create yourself is through the clothes and accessories with which you adorn yourself. So wear your favorite outfits, each and every moment this week. As you do, you may discover that when you love what you wear, not to hide behind, but rather to express who you are, that you tap more fully into the creative energy of the universe and you become your greatest work of art.

How to Do It

Day 1: Love everything you wear today. Put on the sexy underwear you've been saving, or wear that goofy-looking tie your child picked out all by himself as a Father's Day gift. Enjoy the soft, worn denim of your very favorite jeans. Cuddle up in your terrycloth robe when you step out of the shower. Wear that hat you love that you feel a bit shy about actually wearing. Notice how you feel as you go through your day when you love everything you are wearing.

Day 2: Go shopping. This isn't about buying—this is about playing and experimenting. Try on those clothes you always wanted to buy but thought you didn't have enough money for, or were not the right weight or shape for, or didn't have a reason to wear. And as part of your shopping adventure, buy one thing that is truly an expression of the artist, the lover of life that you are.

Day 3: Wear something you have been saving. As you take it out of your closet or drawer, know that this is the special day you have been saving this special item for. Feel the fabric, see the color, admire the style. As you put it on, allow the feeling of abundance and beauty this favorite item symbolizes to infuse your being, and connect fully and deeply with the special being you are as you wear your something special.

Day 4: Go through your closets and drawers and separate the things you love from the things you don't. It is time to let go of all the clothes that no longer are a clear reflection of the beautiful, handsome, loving being you are. The clothes that no longer make your heart sing may very well strike up the band when someone else puts them on. Bring them to a consignment shop, donate them to a homeless shelter, or offer them to friends. If there are some items that you know you will never wear again, but looking at them makes your heart sing, consider hanging them on the wall as art, or cut them up and make a quilt!

Day 5: Now that your closets and drawers are filled only with clothing you love, create a new outfit. Combine clothes you haven't combined before. Wear that bright color to work. Take a risk and wear the shirt you love to spice up your dark suit. Be aware that others may comment on the creativity that you are expressing. When you get a compliment, accept it.

Day 6: Dress up for dinner, use the good dishes, and invite friends over requesting that they wear their favorite outfit. Notice how you feel surrounded by people and things you love, wearing clothes you love.

Day 7: Wear a favorite outfit as you reflect on and write your response to the following questions:

- What did you learn about yourself?
- How do you feel when you love what you wear?
- How does wearing your favorite outfit enhance your living a wholehearted life?

One Day, Some Day, Tomorrow

From the time I was a pre-teen growing up in Manhattan, I looked in magazines and store windows, people-watched, and fantasized, daydreaming that one day I would dress like that. Someday I would be beautiful; tomorrow I would have the perfect wardrobe.

There were times when I had glimpses of that experience. When I was complimented on a dress or an outfit, particularly by a man, I'd go on a major eating binge, often lasting months. I felt so uncomfortable by this positive attention that was out of sync with my beliefs about myself, even though I craved it so deeply. Eventually, there I was in my fifties, repeating the well-worn phrases: *one day I will dress like that, someday I will be beautiful, tomorrow I will get the perfect wardrobe;* yearning to be beautiful and certain that I wasn't.

Through all the decades this was going on, I was also coming to know that we are all creators made in the image of a Loving Creator, and that our creations begin with our thoughts, charged with emotional energy. One day it occurred to me that if I truly wanted to be beautiful, it was time to have new thoughts and to have faith in those new thoughts. So my journey unfolded. The wait was over. One day, the elusive *someday*, was headed for today.

How do you change a thought, how do you live into a new thought, how do you embody a new thought? The starting point is to wake up to your current thoughts. Are these thoughts a reflection of the change you are ready to make? If they aren't, then consciously make up new thoughts that are aligned with your dreams. Let me tell you about the day my new thoughts about myself began to blossom.

I apprenticed with don Miguel Ruiz, who wrote the popular and powerful bestseller *The Four Agreements*. Eighty of us met with him for the weekend every three to five weeks. On the first weekend I noticed Tatyana. She is beautiful. She basks in her beauty. She describes herself as exotically feminine—a current-day Goddess. She dresses beautifully. She and I connected. I have always had beautiful girlfriends, but I simply thought that they were beautiful and I wasn't. In the arena of beauty, we were unequal. Men would notice them and not me. There was no competition between us, as I was clearly not in their league. I felt badly about this, but I figured this was just the way it was. Being beautiful for me, if it was even possible, would happen one day, someday, tomorrow—not today. And there were so many requirements for that day that the list was too long for me to even know all the categories. Some of them were: *when I'm the right weight, when I exercise regularly, when I have a boyfriend, when my nails are all the perfect length, when my hair looks a certain way, when the moon is in a certain position, when the rainfall is a particular number of inches, when I have a certain amount of money in my bank account,* and on and on and on.

On our second weekend with don Miguel, Tatyana and I had an intimate conversation and connected again. The next weekend we were together I woke early on Sunday morning. My air mattress and sleeping bag were next to Tatyana's. As I noticed her asleep next to me, I began having a conversation with her in my mind. I said, "Tatyana, you are so beautiful, you dress so beautifully, you seem comfortable being beautiful—would you go clothes shopping with me?" The next thing I knew, Tatyana was awake and said good morning to me. I told her that I had just been talking to her in my mind, and I repeated the words aloud that I had said in the silence of my thoughts. She smiled and said that she'd love to go shopping with me. I was moving toward *today*!

The next week during a phone coaching session with Rita, who was teaching with don Miguel, I told Rita that I had asked Tatyana to go shopping with me for a new wardrobe. I told her that the wait was over, that I was ready to be beautiful, to take the beauty I felt on the inside and show it on the outside. She said, "I asked Tatyana to go shopping with me also." We checked our schedules, I called Tatyana, and we made a date for our Power Journey Shopping Extravaganza: July 10, 2001. She gave me an assignment to go through magazines and cut out examples of what beauty looks like to me in clothes, without limiting myself by thinking *I could never wear that*. As July 10 approached, some doubts echoed in my mind, and I wondered if I would find anything to buy. Would anything I loved fit me? Would I be disappointed? Would Rita be beautiful and have a successful day, while I wouldn't? When I heard those thoughts, I acknowledged them: "Thank you fear, for voicing your worries. I am choosing new thoughts." And I made up new thoughts: *I have a beautiful wardrobe, Tatyana and Rita are cheerleaders, God is my partner in this, and I* am *beautiful*.

On July 10, 2001, Rita and I drove to Fashion Valley in San Diego to meet Tatyana. We decided to meet in

Macy's. I noticed I had judgments about Macy's—although I imagined that it had a large clothing selection, I thought it was too middle-of-the-road for my transformation! Tatyana got right to work, pointing out the difference between colors that are enhancers to Rita's and my natural coloring and those that are distractors. We learned fast and decided to pick out some things in Macy's to get an idea of what might work. We weren't committed to buying anything this first go-round—we were simply getting clearer about what enhances our beauty. It was a Tuesday morning, and we were the only people in the dressing room.

Tatyana and Rita both told me that the pale-green silk beaded skirt and top looked great on me and that I had to buy them. When I looked in the mirror, all I saw was how fat I was. They told me I didn't look fat at all. I knew that my eyes were seeing what they were used to seeing, and that I needed some help. I asked Tatyana to describe to me what she saw when she looked at me in this green outfit. I was really asking her to help me see myself differently. She said, "If I saw you walking into a room dressed in this outfit I would think: There is a beautiful woman, comfortable in her beauty. She is graceful, creative, and confident. She is open to expressing her beauty in the way she dresses and to being her beauty." That sounded good to me. Rita and I both decided to buy some of the clothes we had tried on. I went to pay for mine and discovered that if I opened a charge account, I could get 10 percent off, and that many of the items cost less than their already marked-down prices. The clothes, the process, and the saleswoman were all conspiring and assisting me to step into *today*. While I was paying, Tatyana and Rita discovered a sale rack on which everything was 65 percent off, and Rita came toward me with an armload of new clothes to try on. I went to that rack, and along with Tatyana, found more beautiful clothes to try on. Every cell of my being was saying *yes*—and the clearer the *yes*, the more there was to take into the dressing room.

Round two in the dressing room: I put on a pair of British tan pants. I put a top over my head, a dark green top that felt like cashmere and embraced my body in its sensual feel. As I arranged the turtleneck and looked into the mirror, the me I had yearned for, the me I had hoped would one day, someday, tomorrow be there, was looking at me. She was my reflection in the mirror. She was smiling, she was beautiful, she was me, and I *saw* her. In the sacred cathedral of Macy's, the store where I got my Girl Scout uniform as a child, magic was happening. The wait was over. I am beautiful, and I am sharing my beauty today, and today, and today.

Warning

by Jenny Joseph

When I am an old woman I shall wear purple
With a red hat which doesn't go, and doesn't suit me.
And I shall spend my pension on brandy and summer
     gloves
And satin sandals, and say we've no money for butter.
I shall sit down on the pavement when I'm tired
And gobble up samples in shops and press alarm bells
And run my stick along the public railings
And make up for the sobriety of my youth.
I shall go out in my slippers in the rain
And pick flowers in other people's gardens
And learn to spit.

You can wear terrible shirts and grow more fat
And eat three pounds of sausages at a go
Or only bread and pickle for a week
And hoard pens and pencils and beermats and things
     in boxes.

But now we must have clothes that keep us dry
And pay our rent and not swear in the street
And set a good example for the children.
We must have friends to dinner and read the papers.
But maybe I ought to practice a little now?
So people who know me are not too shocked and
     surprised
When suddenly I am old, and start to wear purple.

WEEK 18
Acknowledge Accomplishments

To be yourself in a world that is constantly trying to make you something else is the greatest accomplishment.

—RALPH WALDO EMERSON

Acknowledging accomplishments is an important element of the creative process. In 1982, when I studied with Robert Fritz, author of *The Path of Least Resistance*, I learned about the importance of acknowledging accomplishments. He described the creative process as having the following three components:

- *Germination*—an inner process where the seed of an idea is planted in the fertile soil of your consciousness (the idea for this book, for example)
- *Assimilation*—when you begin to see the fruits of the seeds you have germinated in your life (a

book proposal is written; the proposal is sent to publishers; a book contract is signed; the manuscript is completed and sent to the publisher)

- *Completion*—acknowledgement of the completion of the creation (Yippee, I completed my book proposal; I'm so glad my friends spoke with their publisher about taking a look at my proposal; YES, I have a book contract; YAY, my book is a New York Times bestseller; thank you God, Loving Power of the Universe, for guiding my way, Hooray.)

He told us that in his research on composers, all of whom had the artistic and technical skills to compose music, the difference between the ones who were successful and the ones who were not was that successful composers went through all three steps of the creative process. Some composers had creative ideas and stopped there; others had ideas and took action; but it was the people who had ideas, took action, and acknowledged their accomplishments who experienced success.

Don't you feel good when you acknowledge your accomplishments? Yet many of us are not skilled at doing this. We have more practice focusing our attention on what didn't work or what is still undone. We acknowledge, but what we acknowledge is what is lacking.

Think about it. Have you ever completed ten items on your daily to-do list and found yourself at the end of the day thinking only about the two you didn't complete? This drains your energy. When you focus on and acknowledge your accomplishments, the *force* is with you. This *force* energizes you to move with grace and ease through whatever task or project is before you. You feel alive and good about who you are.

Not only does acknowledging your accomplishments enhance your personal well-being, it contributes loving energy to the collective consciousness of peace and happiness for the world. In each and every moment, you have 100 percent power to be aware of and to choose the thoughts you think and where you focus your attention. So this week, acknowledge your accomplishments. This is a week for celebration—isn't every week?

How to Do It

Day 1: At the end of the day, write down five things you have accomplished. Do this every day this week, and whenever you are questioning your ability to get things done or feeling blue. This exercise is less about the items themselves and more about seeing yourself through the eyes of accomplishment. For some of you, this will be like wearing new glasses: You may not be used to them at first, but suddenly your vision clears.

Day 2: Choose an Accomplishment Symbol (a concept based on Robert Fritz's Symbolic Gesture). An Accomplishment Symbol is something that you normally do each day that you endow with the power to represent an accomplishment. Your Accomplishment Symbol may be brushing your teeth, washing your face, shaving, having breakfast, or getting out of bed. Remember, it is something you are already doing, *not* something you think you should be doing.

Since 1982, my Accomplishment Symbol has been brushing my teeth. The association between accomplishment and brushing my teeth is now so strong that I begin and end the day feeling a sense of accomplishment simply by brushing my teeth. Even if it is just a glimmer on some days, the energy of accomplishment is still there. There have been days when just getting the toothbrush to my mouth felt like a major effort. So I would just wet it a bit, without even using toothpaste, and still I would think, "Well, I brushed my teeth today; I accomplished something!"

Day 3: Use self-talk (you talking to you) to acknowledge your accomplishments. You might look in the mirror and say: "Good for me today! I wrote, exercised at the gym, and prepared the material for the class I am teaching tomorrow." While waiting in line at the supermarket, you might say to yourself: "I got a lot done today: I sent a birthday gift to my Mom, I paid my bills, and I am getting the weekly supermarket shopping done right now." While you are on hold on the phone, you might say to yourself: "I've accomplished a lot today. I went to the barber, I saw my son's school play, and I spoke with the mortgage broker about refinancing our mortgage at a lower rate."

Day 4: Brag to three people about your accomplishments.

Day 5: Give yourself a treat to celebrate your accomplishments. It may be a bouquet of flowers, a book you've wanted to read, a massage, a tie that makes you smile, or a bubble bath—your celebration is limited only by your imagination.

Day 6: Acknowledge something of value in each encounter you have today. See everything you do today through the eyes of accomplishment. Sometimes when I am stuck in traffic and on the verge of giving the steering wheel of my life over to impatience, I remind myself of this great opportunity to practice patience, and I acknowledge myself for turning a traffic jam lemon into lemonade. Becoming the greatest lemonade maker in the world is a sure way to add sweetness to your day.

Day 7: Reflect and write your response to the following questions:

- What did you accomplish?
- What did you learn?
- How can you keep your accomplishment muscle firm, strong, flexible, and well toned? Do it.

WEEK 19
Meditate

Meditation can be considered a technique, or practice. It usually involves concentrating on an object, such as a flower, a candle, a sound or word, or the breath. Over time, the number of random thoughts occurring diminishes. More importantly, your attachment to these thoughts, and your identification with them, progressively becomes less.

—DINU ROMAN

Meditation is a practice to quiet your mind. It involves both focus and detachment. We live in a world of sensory overload. I am often astonished at some TV programs that include one or more people talking, a ticker at the bottom of the screen reporting a different story, and sometimes a picture-within-a-picture of something else. This is more input than I care to be bombarded with!

With all the input coming at you and all the electronic devices you have become dependent on, it's not surprising that you are unaware of your thoughts—keeping in mind that 90 to 95 percent of your thoughts are housed in your subconscious. Meditation allows you to calm your mind, turn away from outside stimulation, turn within, and consciously focus your attention. When you do this, you experience a greater sense of relaxation, clarity, and connection with pure consciousness and the Source Energy of the universe. Living life fully requires a direct, conscious connection with your inner experience to which meditation opens a door.

While there are many forms of meditation, it usually involves focusing your attention on your breath, a word, a mantra, or an object, like a candle flame or a flower. Whenever your mind wanders, gently bring it back to the focal point of your mediation. (This is good advice for whatever you are doing—playing golf, working on a creative project, or spending time with your loved ones.) This creates the twofold practice of focusing your attention and detaching from thoughts when they capture your attention.

So often in our lives, rather than witnessing our thoughts and choosing where to place our attention, we give our thoughts free rein. Since our thoughts are magnets that attract our experiences, many of us wind up on a horse that is out of control. Meditation offers the practice of noticing our thoughts and detaching from them. When applied in your daily life, meditation gives you greater power over where you consciously focus your attention and a deeper sense of peace and happiness, passion and purpose.

How to Do It

Day 1: If you are new to meditation, meditate for two periods of ten minutes each. If you are familiar with meditation, meditate for two periods of twenty minutes each. Use the following instructions:

- Sit cross-legged on the floor or comfortably on a chair, with your spine straight and your feet flat on the floor. Place your forearms and hands comfortably on your thighs, palms facing up, and close your eyes.
- Focus your attention on your in-breath and out-breath.
- When your mind wanders, gently turn your attention to your breath. Do this for the entire time you are meditating.

No matter what thoughts hook your attention, return your attention to your breath. When I first began meditating, I would direct my attention to my breath if I noticed I was focused on any of the following thoughts: "This is so uncomfortable." "When is this going to be over?" "I hate this." But if my attention was hooked by thoughts about vacation plans, making love, my dream house, redecorating my bedroom, planting my garden, or anything pleasurable, I would forget to gently bring my attention to my breath, and later I would tell myself, "Well, these are good thoughts to be thinking." I can still remember the moment it occurred to me to gently focus my attention on my breath no matter what the content of my thoughts!

At the end of your mediation time, notice how you

are feeling. At the end of the day reflect on the impact the two mediation sessions had on your experience of your day.

Day 2: Repeat the meditation from Day 1, focusing on your breath for twenty minutes twice during the day. If you are new to meditation aim to add more time each day, until you reach twenty minutes. Arrange to attend a meditation class. Though there are many resources for doing this online, I encourage you to actually attend a class. Look up meditation on the internet, or call a local Buddhist *zendo* or yoga center for information about meditation groups in your area. Remember, you don't have to sign up for life. Simply explore and experiment. Go to your local library and get a book on meditation, then read it and practice the exercises. Explore meditation audio and videos online.

Day 3: Do a twenty-minute walking meditation today. As you walk slowly, focus your attention on each step. When you bring your left foot forward, say the word *left* in your mind, and when you bring your right foot forward, say the word *right* in your mind. If you lose track and are saying *left* in your mind as your right foot is moving forward, gently make the adjustment, aligning your body mind spirit. Take each step slowly and mindfully. If you are unable to walk, repeat the meditation instructions from Day 1.

Day 4: Create a meditation space in your home. This may be a room of your own that is your sanctuary, or simply a chair or pillow on the floor. Be creative. You may want to have artwork, special objects, a candle, incense, or photos of loved ones surrounding you, or a simple altar with objects that are sacred to you. You may want a book of inspiring quotations nearby that you can read before or after your meditation. If you travel frequently, consider creating a portable altar you can set up wherever you are, that evokes a sacred meditation space for you.

Day 5: Meditate twice today in your meditation space. Choose the meditation format of your choice for two twenty-minute periods.

Day 6: Do a breathing mediation or walking meditation for twenty minutes. For your second twenty-minute meditation practice, use a candle flame or flower as the focal point for your attention, keeping your eyes open.

Day 7: Meditate once today. After you have meditated, reflect and write your response to the following questions. Remember, there is no right answer; this exercise is to wake you up to the present moment.

- What did you experience while meditating today? This week?
- What do you feel during and immediately after meditating?
- How did a daily meditation practice impact your day?
- What is your commitment and plan for incorporating a meditation practice into your daily life?

> To integrate meditation in action is the whole
> ground and point and purpose of meditation.
> —THE TIBETAN BOOK
> OF LIVING AND DYING

WEEK 20

Be a Visitor in Your Town

Being a visitor in your town is a wonderful way to reac-
quaint yourself with the place where you live. It gives
you the opportunity to see with fresh eyes those places
that have disappeared into the background. Being
a visitor also enhances our experience of the present
moment by helping us pay attention to where we are,
when we are there. So often in our human experience
our mind is one place, our body another place, our
spirit is off on its own, and our consciousness is focused
in the past or future. A wholehearted life requires
being aligned in body mind spirit and appreciating the
moment. This week, be a visitor in your town, really

see where you live, appreciate it—its beauty, diversity, colors, fragrances, sounds, familiarity—and discover it anew.

How to Do It

Day 1: Take a new route and notice what you see. If you always go to the right when you come out of your driveway or apartment building, go to the left today. Take the stairs rather than the elevator. Take a bus rather than the subway. Walk rather than drive. Turn off your phone. Listen to the sounds in your world when you take this new route and notice what you see. Actually be where you are, when you are there. Stop and smell the flowers in the flower box of the store you pass. Notice the stores in your neighborhood. *See* the neighborhood that you call home.

Day 2: Look in your local newspaper or online at the listings of community and cultural events for the week, and make plans to do something new, or at least something you haven't done for a while. Go to an opening at an art gallery. Go to the opera. Attend a community planning meeting. Take a cooking class. Be a member of your community, and while you are participating in this activity, talk with two people you haven't spoken with before. Remember, act as if you are a visitor in your town and be open to new experiences.

Day 3: Get to know your neighborhood merchants. Go into a store you usually shop in and a store you haven't been in before and chat with the people working there. You might do this in your supermarket. Go to a checkout line with a checker you don't know and have a conversation. Focus your conversation on something you appreciate or a question you have *as a visitor*. Remember, the purpose of this is to experience greater connection, peace, and happiness, so don't complain about long lines or lousy weather!

Day 4: Today, be a visitor in your house or apartment. If you always sit at a particular seat at the dining room table, switch. If you usually sit in a particular chair, move the chair to another place in the room or sit somewhere else. Tonight sleep on a different side of the bed. Again, be awake and aware of your surroundings. See your home through eyes of appreciation. Experience your home anew. If you notice that you are dissatisfied with where you live and mainly focus on what you don't like, then make some changes. Buy a bouquet of flowers or a new plant. Change the furniture around. Be a visitor in your home as if this is a desired location you have been eager to visit.

Day 5: Look at a local map and plan an exploration of your town. Go to a park you have never gone to before. Drive through a part of your town that you are unfamiliar with. Plan excursions down new streets to places you have never been before.

Day 6: Today, expand your experience of being a visitor and play with the idea of being a visitor to Planet Earth. What are the customs you notice? What are the costumes people wear? What do they eat? What language do they speak? What do you notice when you are a visitor on Planet Earth?

Day 7: Write or e-mail your local paper or chamber of commerce expressing your appreciation for your town. Reflect and write your response to the following questions:

- How did acting as if you were a visitor change your perspective of where you live?
- What did you learn about your town?
- How do your feel about your town after being a visitor for a week?
- How can you continue to experience your town and your home as great places to be?

A Visit to New York

I was born and raised in New York City. I live in eastern Long Island now and most often go to New York City when I have something specific planned to do there. I am comfortable in Manhattan and know my way around. Often because of this familiarity I don't visit when I go there. I do what I have to do, see friends, and go home. Last week I was a visitor. I sat on the bus looking out the windows, noticing the magnificent greens of the new leaves on the trees. I stood in the Times Square area in awe of the neon signs—particularly the one, high above the others, that read, "Imagine all the people living life in peace." Slowly I turned, looking in one direction after the other. The beauty of this creation inspired me. The sound of steel drums, the amazing hip-hop dancing, the musicians from Bolivia were spectacular street theater. Being a visitor, that simple shift in perspective, is the best way to be wherever I am. Being open to new sights actually invites new sights, new experiences. My heart was happy.

WEEK 21
Hug

Heartfelt

Unconditional

Gratitude

—SUSAN IVORY

Hugs are an expression of love and support. Sometimes you give a hug when you have an irresistible impulse of delight and love that you want to express physically. Other hugs are a warm, caring embrace that let the people you are hugging know that you are there for them, that they are not alone. And some hugs are expressions of passion, a sensual, sexual embrace.

We live in a culture that has taboos about touching and hugging. We can hug family and close friends, but in the workplace it may not be okay to hug a coworker unless there is a good reason for it, such as their going-away party! Sometimes we hold back from hugging because we worry about what the other person will think. Sometimes we hold back because we don't want to intrude, and sometimes we hold back simply from lack of hugging practice. Sometimes we don't ask for a hug because we are afraid of being rejected, or we worry about imposing on someone, or we're concerned that this physical contact may be misinterpreted. Hugs are a natural part of living a wholehearted life. They say, "I love you. I care for you. I'm here for you." This week, *hug*—when you feel the urge to ask for a hug, ask for it and receive it.

How to Do It

Day 1: Give ten hugs today. Notice how you hug. Do you get right in there and allow yourself to fully give and receive? Do you hold back, unsure of the "right way" to do this? Who is it easy for you to hug? Who are you hesitant to hug?

Day 2: Ask for and receive ten hugs today. Notice what this experience is like for you. What did you learn about yourself and hugging?

Day 3: Send a long-distance hug to a loved one. You may call her on the phone with an "I love you" message. You may Skype and tell him to take a moment to feel the virtual hug. Be creative and let the person know that you are sending a hug her way.

Day 4: Visit the Georgia Girl Hugs Web site at www. gagirl.com/hugs/hug.html. Then, write a poem, essay, or song about the importance of hugs.

Day 5: Hug yourself five times today. You can actually wrap your arms around yourself and allow yourself to feel you embracing you. Hug yourself by taking care of yourself. If you are blue and need a hug of encouragement, rent that favorite movie and feel it hugging you as you snuggle up and watch it. If you are delighted with yourself, hug your fingernails with glittery nail polish. Be creative about hugging yourself today.

Day 6: Write about what holds you back from giving, asking for, and receiving hugs. What new thoughts can you have that would make this expression of love easier for you? If hugs are a challenge for you, imagine that you are a person who easily gives and receives hugs and make up thoughts that make hugging easy. Create a new story about you being the most fabulous hugger on earth. With three people today, be the most fabulous hugger on earth.

Day 7: Reflect and write your response to the following questions:

- What did you learn about yourself?
- How can you spread hugs around?

Hugs

by Jill Wolf

There's something in a simple hug
That always warms the heart;
It welcomes us back home
And makes it easier to part.

A hug's a way to share the joy
And sad times we go through,
Or just a way for friends to say
They like you 'cause you're you.

Hugs are meant for anyone
For whom we really care,
From your grandma to your neighbor,
Or a cuddly teddy bear.

A hug is an amazing thing—
It's just the perfect way
To show the love we're feeling
But can't find the words to say.

It's funny how a little hug
Makes everyone feel good;
In every place and language,
It's always understood.

And hugs don't need new equipment,
Special batteries or parts—
Just open up your arms
And open up your hearts.

We need 4 hugs a day for survival.
We need 8 hugs a day for maintenance.
We need 12 hugs a day for growth.

—VIRGINIA SATIR

WEEK 22
Be Kind

This is my simple religion. There is no need for temples; no need for complicated philosophy. Our own brain, our own heart is our temple; the philosophy is kindness.

—THE DALAI LAMA

Being kind to ourselves and to others, including all of life, is a treasure that is always available for us to give. It doesn't require great wealth, large blocks of time, or a complicated procedure. It is the way you care for and love yourself and others. It is a point of view, a filter through which you view the world—ah yes, often considered to be rose-colored!

Kindness is expressed in our thoughts, words, and actions. Being kind can be as simple as saying "Thank you" to the cashier at your local supermarket after you have paid for your groceries. It may involve traveling far to be with a friend in need, paying the toll for the car behind you, or saying a prayer for people involved in a news story of suffering. Being kind is how we apply the Golden Rule, *Do unto others as you would have others do unto you.* In the scriptures of each of the world's religions, there is a version of the Golden Rule, also known as the ethic of reciprocity.

Your personal experience of wholehearted living is dependent upon kindness. And the possibility of peace in our families, workplaces, communities, institutions— in the world—requires that we be kind to one another, remembering that we are all connected and that what is done to any part affects the whole.

Kindness has a ripple effect, often greater than the act itself. Imagine a world where spontaneous acts of kindness are a given. The receiver is happy, surprised, and often wakes up to the present moment. When the recipient of this kindness tells this story to others, the kindness extends outward and seeds the idea of being kind in those who hear about it. Since the energy of loving-kindness moves through you as you express kindness, often the greatest benefit from random acts of kindness is experienced by the giver.

This week, to deepen and expand your open-heartedness, be kind. When you feel an inner prompting to offer a helping hand, do it. New patterns of behavior usually feel awkward at first, so if you notice you are feeling a bit shy and embarrassed about doing a good deed, do it anyway!

How to Do It

Day 1: Be kind to yourself today in your thoughts, words, and actions. Anytime you notice you are being critical or judgmental of yourself in your thoughts or words, change those thoughts and words. If you have a deadline to meet at work and one of your coworkers has stopped by to shoot the breeze, be kind to yourself by gently asserting yourself, saying you have work to do and will have to cut the conversation short. Treat yourself as though you are precious, because you are.

Day 2: Make a Kindness List to help remind you of the various faces of kindness. Here are some ideas to start your list:

- Help someone carry their groceries
- Pay the toll for the car behind you
- Call family members or friends and tell them how special they are to you
- Anonymously leave chocolate kisses on your coworkers' desks, or give one to the supermarket cashier
- Leave a thank-you note for your mail carrier
- Donate a pint of blood
- Drop some loose change on the street for someone to find

Day 3: Be kind. Perform one act of kindness for everyone you meet today. Smiles and thank-yous can go a long way. Since I believe that thoughts are real things and that we can express our kindness through our thoughts, often when I am waiting for a bus I will send one of the following thoughts to everyone who passes me (and in New York City that's a lot of people!):

- God loves you
- You are love
- You live in a loving world
- Your gifts and talents are a blessing—share them

When I do this, my heart opens, and I take a moment to actually see the people who are passing directly through my world.

Day 4: Read the book or see the movie *Pay It Forward* and then pay it forward.

Day 5: Customize your screen saver and put sticky notes around your house and workplace with quotations reminding you to be kind. Here are some to choose from, or be creative and make up your own:

- *Remember there's no such thing as a small act of kindness. Every act creates a ripple with no logical end.* —SCOTT ADAMS
- *Forget injuries, never forget kindnesses.* —AESOP
- *No act of kindness, however small, is ever wasted.* —AESOP
- *Little deeds of kindness, little words of love, Help to make earth happy like the heaven above.* —JULIA A. FLETCHER CARNEY

Day 6: Talk with five people today about the power of being kind.

Day 7: Reflect and write your response to the following questions:

- What did you learn this week by consciously practicing being kind?
- How can you incorporate kindness into your daily life? Do it.

Just because an animal is large, it doesn't mean he doesn't want kindness; however big Tigger seems to be, remember that he wants as much kindness as Roo.

—*POOH'S LITTLE*
INSTRUCTION BOOK,
INSPIRED BY A. A. MILNE

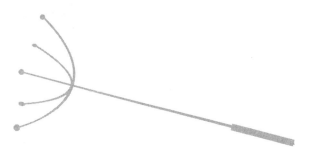

Being Kind

It was a beautiful summer afternoon. I was driving in my fire-engine-red Miata convertible, with my gray-and-white sheepdog, Rosie, in the passenger seat, moving at sixty-five miles per hour. As I slowed down, approaching the tollbooth, I had to move into the long cash line to pay my toll, since I didn't have an E-ZPass in my car. I was moving at a snail's pace. As I sat there, holding Rosie with my right hand, and my toll in my left hand, I heard that still small voice within say, "Pay the toll for the people behind you." I thought, "I don't know if I want to do that. Well, it would be a random act of kindness; it would be a nice thing to do." I started feeling embarrassed about doing this random act of kindness. "What would the people behind me think? What would the toll taker think?" Then I thought, "What does it matter what they think?" I had made a commitment to listen to and follow the instructions of that still small voice within. So, continuing to hold Rosie, I reached into my wallet and got more money, preparing to pay the toll for the car behind me.

There were still about seven cars in front of me, so I started gazing into my rearview mirror to see who was in the car behind me. There were a man, a woman, and a child in the car. I began to fantasize about what their reaction would be when they drove to the tollbooth and the attendant told them that their toll had already been paid. I thought they would be happy. I imagined them with smiles on their faces, telling their family and friends about discovering, as they drove through the tollbooth, that their toll had already been paid. So I was feeling good about this random act of kindness I was ready to perform, when all of a sudden, on my right, a pickup truck started cutting in front of me. Instantly I was transformed. What did this guy think he was doing cutting in front of me? I was in line in front of him! I held fast to my position, not letting that big pickup truck edge me out in my little Miata. "I'll show him," I thought.

Well, in the process of showing him, it wound up that the pickup truck became the car behind me! What was I going to do now, faced with this enormous dilemma? Would I still perform the random act of kindness? Would I reinforce his behavior after he had attempted to cut me off? Through my irritated chatter, I again heard that still small voice within, saying calmly and clearly, "Pay the toll for the car behind you. Pay the toll for the car behind you." As I went through the tollbooth, I paid my toll and the toll for the car behind me.

As I wrote this story, I was reminded that oftentimes I want to negotiate with God, with the still small voice within. I want to decide whom I'll be kind to. The challenge, for me, is simply to listen to and follow the instructions of that still small voice within when I am prompted to be kind.

WEEK 23

Live Abundantly

Life is a banquet and most people are starving.

—AUNTIE MAME

Living abundantly begins with a perspective, a point of view. So often we think that our abundance is determined by the material possessions we have. We will be abundant when we have a new car, a new house, the latest electronic gadgets, or a bigger income. Then we get a new car, a new house, a new electronic gadget, and a salary increase, and rather than feeling prosperous and abundant, all we notice are increased monthly bills, or we worry that these new things that we desired will break down or won't last. In the midst of receiving what we thought was our heart's desire, our thoughts continue to focus on lack. Each time a new desire surfaces, instead of greeting it with open arms and faith in our creative ability, we get lost in the dissatisfaction of what is missing.

In order to live abundantly, you must have an inner experience of abundance, prosperity, love, and joy that is independent of the things you have. I recently saw a quote that captures this idea: "If you want to make more money then you have to decide to be worth more." It highlights that your experience of abundance and prosperity begins in your consciousness.

As you read this, you may notice a voice within you asking, "Then why are people starving? Why do some people have more than others?" A usual way to address questions like this is to talk about power, government, economics, greed, the unfairness of the world, and powerful people who take advantage of the weak, such as business executives who have inside information and sell their stock at high profits before the general public gets the information. When you think about these situations, it's easy to rely on the tried and assumed true beliefs about the world being unfair, or that you can't trust government or the wealthy, or that people are just plain greedy. When you focus your attention on lack, unfairness, and greed in the world rather than on abundance, your thoughts contribute to this lack. It is easy to find evidence of lack if that is your point of view. It is just as easy to see evidence of abundance if that is your lens of perception. This is not about denying the full range of expression of creation on earth; it is about using your power to focus your attention on the abundant world you desire and believing that your creative power is real. All we actually have control over is what we think and where we direct our attention. Whether or not you believe this, experiment and see what you discover. Notice the change in your personal world and in how you see the global community when you focus your attention on living abundantly.

How to Do It

Day 1: Complete the following statement as fully as possible: An abundant person believes _____. Write as many statements as you can think of. After you have written your responses, make sure that each item supports what an abundant person *is* rather than what she or he is *not*. Some examples are:

- An abundant person trusts in the universe to support his desires, *rather than* an abundant person doesn't worry about his desires being met.
- An abundant person acknowledges her accomplishments each step of the way, *rather than* an abundant person doesn't focus on what is not working.

Now rewrite the list in the first person:

- I trust the universe to support my desires.
- I acknowledge my accomplishments each step of the way.

Read your list aloud each morning when you wake up, at night before you go to sleep, and whenever your personal programming needs an abundance *zap*. When you start to read it, first say your intention: "I am installing my new and improved abundance programming."

Day 2: Make a list of the riches in your life right now. If you want abundance in your future, the starting place is seeing and experiencing abundance *now*, in your present. Some items on my list are:

- Loving and supportive community of family and friends
- Spiritual, emotional, and physical health and well-being
- Satisfying work
- Gorgeous hair
- Comfortable bed
- Beautiful home
- Loving partner
- Delicious grandchildren
- Strong and flexible muscles
- Healthy teeth and gums
- Well-stocked cupboards
- Great car

Be playful with this list and read it when you need to be reminded of the abundance in your life.

Day 3: Have a written conversation with money today. Start by writing, "Money, I am ready and willing to have a loving relationship with you. Please help me so I can treat you as my money honey." Write money's response and continue the conversation until you feel a loving relationship with money. Remember, if you want money to be the best it can be for you, then you have to be the best you that you can be. You have to commit to living your wholehearted life.

Day 4: Buy yourself something special today. This is not about cost; this is about buying something that symbolizes abundance in your life. It may be a download of that new song that gave you the chills, a bouquet of flowers, or a single rose. You may order the sandwich that you really want but don't usually order because it is three dollars more than the other sandwiches on the menu. Act as if you are abundant today and be abundant today.

Day 5: Be generous. True generosity, with no strings attached, expecting nothing in return, and without scorekeeping, is a direct expression of abundance. Be generous with your time and skills by volunteering for something you believe in; leave an extra tip for the wait staff; give away thank-yous. Go through your closet and gather up things you don't wear or use and donate them to a homeless shelter or people in need.

Day 6: Experiment with tithing. There is a universal law of tenfold return. This means that when you give freely, your return is tenfold. You don't give to get the return; you give freely, and what you give flows back to you tenfold. Particularly in terms of money, many of us think the law of attraction doesn't apply. It does. Money is simply energy, and when you allow the energy of abundance to flow through you, then money and other resources continue to flow to you. When you stop the flow of abundance out of fear, anxiety, and worry, the flow of money stops. During the next six months, experiment. Whenever you get money, before you pay any bill, take 10 percent and give it to something you believe in. What is most important is that you give with an open heart.

Day 7: Have a conversation with three people about abundance. Share your ideas about an abundant life, starting with thoughts that support abundance in your life. Reflect and write your response to the following questions:

- What did you learn about your relationship with abundance this week?
- How does your experience with abundance relate to living a wholehearted life?
- What are the most powerful thoughts to believe in order to experience abundance and prosperity in all the arenas of your life?

Abundance and Me

My life is abundant. From the outside it has always looked that way, but for many years it didn't seem that way to me. I focused on what I didn't have and worried that I wouldn't get what I really wanted. When I got it, there was always something else to want, so I didn't really enjoy anything I'd gotten. In 1997, from the outside, my life looked enviable. I was married to a local celebrity in my high-profile community. I was part of a large family. I lived in a house with a view of majestic sunsets on the bay. I drove a fire-engine-red sports car. I had a lucrative consulting practice, and I made my own hours. I traveled first class on airplanes, stayed in the best hotels in the world, and had dinner with celebrities. I wore a big diamond ring and got a mink coat for a Valentine's Day gift. My bills were paid. I knew interesting people and had loving friends. A housekeeper kept my house. My office, a beautiful sanctuary, had been built just for me.

But I was miserable, as nothing ever seemed to be enough for me. I was angry, and I blamed my husband, my stepkids, and mostly myself for not being pretty enough, sexy enough, thin enough, good enough, and lovable enough. My life collapsed. My husband decided to divorce me and on the same day was in a new relationship. I was devastated. I decided to approach this crisis as though I had been diagnosed with a terminal illness. I knew that, though I might not physically die, if I didn't change my beliefs I would be like the walking dead. I knew that this would be an inside job. If I didn't change the software of my mind, no matter what I did to the outside, there would be no sustainable change. It was time for me to walk my talk and put all the ideas and skills I had taught others into practice.

With the help of wonderful therapists, teachers, friends, and family, I reinvented myself. I did this by making up a new story about myself and the world in which I live: "I am a Loved and Loving child of a Loving Universe."

Today I see all life through the eyes of wonder. When I hear about suffering, I send prayers of love to that part of the world, and I am grateful for reminders that life is precious and that I need to honor today. Every day there are horror stories of great suffering and hatred in the world. I ask myself, "Okay, how do I view this through the eyes of love?" And I remind myself to be grateful, to be loving, and to have faith that my love and my expressions of love do make a difference.

Abundance is looking through rose-colored glasses to see the gifts that are present in all situations. I remember that every moment is an opportunity to express my love. Every moment is a call for love. Pollyanna is a good role model. Isn't it time to put on your rose-colored glasses?

WEEK 24

Express Your Love

Love doesn't make the world go round. Love is what
makes the ride worthwhile.

—FRANKLIN P. JONES

Expressing your love is the most powerful and precious
gift you have to offer. It can take many forms, as in
simply saying "I love you," or sending flowers or loving
thoughts to someone. During my apprenticeship with
don Miguel Ruiz, the author of *The Four Agreements*,
one day he said, "There are ten million ways to say 'I
love you.'" Since then I have been exploring the variety
of ways I can express my love and the ways in which
others express theirs. What I have learned is that our
love is expressed when we *are* love.

Our natural state is love. Often we forget this and
wait for special occasions to express our love, or for
someone to act in a particular way, or for the circum-

stances to be just perfect. When we wait to express our love, we miss out on the glorious experience of being wholehearted that is always available to us. Truly, the easiest way to express your love is to allow love to flow through you. Here are some ways to do this:

- Think of a person, a place, or an experience you love. Focus your attention on it, using the full resources of your imagination. See it, hear it, smell it, taste it, feel it. Notice what happens. How do you feel? If you allow yourself to surrender to this experience, love will be flowing through you.
- Take a few deep breaths and focus on your heart. Your heart is the place where love lives. Allow yourself to feel the love that is in your heart. Imagine your love as a glorious white light that expands with each in-breath and is given freely with each exhalation.
- Listen to a favorite piece of music, read a poem, smell the intoxicating fragrance of a flower, and allow the beauty to touch your being and help you feel the love that you are.

This week, express your love. Start with your awareness of love moving through you and then move on to giving it away. If you notice you're holding back because you're shy or because some people, in your judgment, don't deserve your love, express it anyway. We are all expressions of God, and God is love. This week, see love in everyone and express your love fully. Remember, if some people don't seem lovable to you, they may have simply forgotten that they are love. Your expression of love may be the reminder they need.

How to Do It

Day 1: Be love. This is a choice. Even if you are in the midst of a crisis in your life, you can choose to connect with the energy of love. Think of people and places you love and allow thoughts of them to fill you with love. Put reminders around your home and office that say "I Am Love." Whether or not you believe this, act as if it is true. When you are love, everything you do is an expression of love.

Day 2: When you are off-center, stressed, frustrated, angry, impatient, experiencing hell, ask yourself the question, "What would love do here?" Listen to the answer and act on it. The answer you receive may not be what your ego thinks is the right thing to do. Do it anyway. Putting your ego in the driver's seat of your life, rather than allowing the wisdom of your loving heart to direct your ego, is what got you in this jam to begin with.

Day 3: Consciously express your love to at least twenty people today. Be creative. You may send a card, a text message, or a voice mail; massage someone's shoulders; help someone carry packages; make a romantic dinner; listen to someone in need. Remember to include yourself in this group of twenty people.

Day 4: Live your day as if you are an emissary of love. You are an angel and the message you have been sent to deliver is that we are love. If you are thinking you're not an emissary of love because you don't have a boyfriend or girlfriend, because you're overweight, because you hate your job, because you are an alcoholic, because you were abused as a child...because, because, because...act as if you are an emissary of love anyway.

Day 5: Notice all the times during the day when you forget that you are love, and as soon as you notice, express your love. When you look at yourself in the mirror and hear yourself saying, "I am ugly," change that thought in the moment, and express your love by having a new thought: "I am love, I am magnificent, I'm great just the way I am at this very moment." If you hear yourself mumbling about your coworker, saying, "He is a jerk," have a new thought and express your love. A simple way to know if you have forgotten that you are love is when you judge yourself or someone else, when you are abusive to yourself or someone else, when you gossip about yourself or someone else, or when you are critical of yourself or someone else. At those times, you are not expressing love.

Day 6: Talk with three people today about being an emissary of love.

Day 7: Write a poem, essay, song or draw a picture that captures being a mighty expression of love. Reflect and write your response to the following questions:

- What did you learn about expressing your love?
- How did you express your love?

WEEK 25

Go on a Media Diet

You are what you watch.

A media diet requires eliminating these activities—social media, newspapers, magazines, TV, radio, music—from your daily schedule. Notice your reaction when you consider this idea. Are you worried that you will miss out on something important? Are you experiencing a sense of loss or deprivation? Are you wondering what this has to do with living a wholehearted life?

This isn't a commitment to eliminate these activities for the rest of your life, although after a week of this diet you may choose to make some changes in your media habits or addictions. The purpose of this diet is twofold:

1. Your experience of wholehearted living is nourished based on where you focus your attention. Some of the activities of the previous weeks have directed your attention to creating a daily ritual, consciously using the creative power of your word, and being kind. This week you are asked to eliminate sources of worry, drama, and anxiety. Much of what is in newspapers, on online news feeds, on the radio (including the words of many songs), and in TV programming ignites anxiety about the present and future. I often hear the word television in my mind as *tell-a-vision* and the vision that is often being told is one that is the exact opposite of whole-hearted living. If you are committed to living a life of passion and purpose, it is important to use your discretion in choosing what you allow into your consciousness. Keep in mind that this is not judging and criticizing what the media reports (remember: the act of criticizing and judging is not an act of love, compassion, and acceptance); this is about making choices about the words, images, and ideas you feed yourself.

2. By going on a media diet, you allow for more silence in your life. Often your mind is filled with the clutter of outside stimulation. You are so used to noise that *you cannot hear yourself think*. Think about it for a moment: How often do you automatically turn on the radio when you get into your car, without consciously choosing what you want to listen to? How often throughout the day are your eyes glued to your smartphone? How often do you turn on the TV/Hulu/Netflix when you walk into your house, or even fall asleep to the sound of a TV program—possibly even the nighttime news, which is often a rehash of the news that has already been

reported earlier in the day? How often do you check your social media in the morning as an automatic habit rather than making a conscious choice in the moment? Think of what it would be like if you gave yourself the opportunity to experience silence. It might actually be quite noisy, at first! It would give you a chance to hear your thoughts and make choices about which thoughts support your intentions and which thoughts feed worry, fear, and anxiety in your life. In silence you have the chance to daydream—and when you daydream that your desires are fully accomplished, you are supporting the creative process of creating the life you want to live.

Enjoy dieting this week, enjoy the silence, listen to the tape of your self-talk and choose thoughts and images that tell-a-vision of love, kindness, and compassion for yourself and others, and notice the weight of anxiety and worry dissolving.

How to Do It
First, prepare for your worries. Going cold turkey on this diet may be uncomfortable.

- If you are worried about missing your favorite TV shows, set your DVR to record them (this may give you a chance to actually learn how to do this!) or add your favorite shows to your Hulu queue. If "chilling out" in front of the TV has been a source of relaxation for you, make a list of other ways you can relax rather than focusing on what you are missing.
- Unplug your TV, DVD, electronic devices, and radio. (Yes, this diet includes watching and

renting movies, too!) Put a "gone fishing" notice on your Facebook and Twitter pages.

- If your daily newspaper is delivered, choose to put it somewhere out of sight. To reduce temptation, cancel delivery for the week.

Day 1: Rather than immediately filling your new free time with activity, experience the silence. Notice how you feel. Listen to your self-talk and have new thoughts if your self-talk is critical, judgmental, or abusive of yourself or others.

Day 2: Make a list of activities and projects you have wanted to begin, complete, or experiment with. Choose one to start today.

Day 3: Notice when you automatically, unconsciously go off your diet. Congratulate yourself for noticing; then get back on it. During the week I was on this diet I was surprised to discover how often I automatically opened my Words with Friends app when I had a spare moment. A friend who was visiting said to me, "I thought you were on a media diet this week." I realized, in that moment, that I had gone off the diet without even noticing! So notice when you just start flipping through a magazine, read the newspaper headlines when you walk past a newsstand, or are seduced by a TV in a restaurant or airport—and remind yourself of your diet.

Day 4: With the increased time you have that is not being filled with outside noise, notice and make a list of your self-talk phrases that are abusive, critical, or judgmental of yourself and others. Next to each item, write phrases that you can turn your attention to when you notice this criticism in the future.

Day 5: Share your experience of being on this diet with three people and notice their reaction.

Day 6: Make a plan for reincorporating media into your life. Here are some parts of my plan:

- No media, other than checking the weather, before I begin my workday.
- No media on my short drives around town when doing errands.
- Choose a media Sabbath one day each week. I look at my schedule at the beginning of each week to select the day.
- Meditate in silence for twenty minutes at least four times a week.

Day 7: Reflect and write your response to the following questions:

- What have you learned about yourself being on a media diet? What was easy? What was challenging?
- What surprised you about being on this diet?
- What adjustments do you want to make in your daily life as a result of this diet?

WEEK 26

Listen to and Follow the Still Small Voice

The Holy Spirit does not scream at us to be heard. He requires that we be quiet to hear his "still small voice." This is such a stretch for us, living as we do in a sound-saturated world. But the rewards—peace, contentment, and a sense of purpose—are well worth the effort.

— KATHY KOCH, PHD

Listening to and following the still small voice is a practice that leads to what seem to be magic and miracles in your daily life. The still small voice is your inner wisdom, your connection with Source Energy, your intuition, God's guidance illuminating your way. When listening to your still small voice, a common challenge is the competition that has its own ideas for the direction you take. This competition is the voice of your ego (EGO can be an acronym for Edging God Out) or the voice of fear (FEAR can be an acronym for Failure Expected And Received).

One starting place for listening to and following the still small voice is your feelings. Your feelings are a magnificent guidance system, your personal GPS, that lets you know if you are experiencing heaven or hell, love or fear, connection or disconnection with Source Energy or God. If you are feeling inspired, content, and loving, you are connected with Source Energy; if you are feeling angry, victimized, vengeful, or alone, you are experiencing a call, to change the channel, and to reconnect with Source Energy.

The still small voice speaks in words, images, promptings that are clear, direct, concise, unemotional, and not necessarily what your rational mind would expect at that moment. It may be as simple as "Make a right turn," when the quickest route would be a left turn, or "Call your mother" when you just spoke with her twenty minutes earlier. The still small voice also speaks to you through a conversation you overhear that resonates deeply, or through the line in a song that gives you an idea that results in a change in your life. This voice is always providing loving guidance. Your work is to listen. The voices of our ego and our fear are filled with emotional static and a whole list of reasons to justify their instructions. These voices are concerned with winning and losing, and with being right.

When you listen to and follow the instructions of the still small voice, you connect more fully with universal energy. In this process, prayers are answered; synchronicities and coincidences flourish. You open yourself to an infinite source of well-being.

For those of you who think that things won't happen unless you do them yourself, unless you control and orchestrate all your relationships and circumstances, this idea of listening to and following the still small voice will seem like a big risk and require a leap of faith.

So for this week, experiment. See what it's like when you ask for, listen to, and follow the still small voice. Then reflect on your experience. And continue to experiment with expanding and deepening your connection with your still small voice everyday.

How to Do It

Day 1: Relax, invite the still small voice to speak to you, and write for fifteen minutes.

- Make yourself comfortable. Have your journal, notebook, or paper and pen nearby or sit in front of your computer.
- Close your eyes and focus on your breath. Breathe in a sense of calm and relaxation and exhale fully and completely. Do this five times.
- On your next out-breath, sigh into the support of the seat beneath your body and the floor beneath your feet.
- Focus your attention on your intention: "I choose to hear my still small voice."
- Focus your attention on your heart, knowing that the still small voice speaks from your heart.
- Listen.
- When you feel ready—trust that you will know when you are ready—begin to write for fifteen minutes. Write whatever comes to mind, even if it's "I don't know what to write." Simply write and know that through this process, you are connecting fully and deeply with your still small voice.
- When you have written for fifteen minutes, notice how you feel.

Day 2: Make yourself comfortable (preferably sitting up), close your eyes, and quiet your mind by focusing your attention on your breath. Think of a situation you would like guidance about and formulate a question. You can choose something that you have been struggling with and worried about, or something as simple as what to cook for dinner tonight. This is an exercise to strengthen your connection with your still small voice. Here are some possible questions to consider:

- How can I be more loving in my relationship with my husband/wife/partner?
- What is the best way for me to approach my boss about a raise?
- What is my heart's desire?
- How can I experience a greater sense of well-being in my life?
- What's the best birthday present for me to buy for my girlfriend?
- How can I be most helpful to my brother-in-law who is struggling with alcoholism?
- What's a great dinner I can make for my family tonight?
- How can I best contribute to life on earth?

Ask your question and then listen to the answer. If you hear something you don't understand, simply ask for clarification. Allow the still small voice to speak while you listen. You may want to write down what you heard to reinforce the message in your consciousness. Acknowledge yourself for asking and listening.

Day 3: Once an hour, in the course of your daily activities, ask for guidance and listen to the response from your still small voice. Follow the guidance. Some questions you might ask are:

- What's the best use of my time right now?
- What do I want for lunch?
- What's the best route to take to get to work?
- Who can I ask for help regarding _____?
- Where did I put my keys?

Allow yourself to play with this. This is a communication exercise that will open you to a source of wisdom that has your best interests in mind. Notice if you want to negotiate with the guidance you are getting, and then follow the guidance anyway!

Day 4: Choose something you would like your still small voice to help you with. Ask for help. Listen to the response and follow the guidance. I was lazy about flossing my teeth and I thought it was important for me to floss—not because I *should*, but because I want to take care of my teeth. I noticed that when it came time to floss at night, I would begin to plead and negotiate. (Who was I negotiating with?) One day, I decided to enlist the help of the still small voice. I asked for a gentle reminder to floss, and I got it. I'd be standing at the bathroom sink, brushing my teeth, and I would hear, "Floss your teeth"—a direct, clear instruction. I thanked the still small voice for the reminder and I flossed. Sometimes, when the reminder comes, I think, *I don't wanna*—and then I remind myself that each time I floss I strengthen the channel of communication with the still small voice and care for my teeth at the same time.

Day 5: Establish a sign between your still small voice and you, between your inner wisdom and your outer life, so you will know when your still small voice is talking with you. Quiet your mind and ask for a sign that represents your inner wisdom. Listen to the answer. In your daily life, when your sign appears, thank your inner wisdom for getting your attention and then follow the instructions.

I often thank the still small voice for speaking loud enough for me to hear and clear enough for me to understand.

Day 6: Use the still small voice to articulate your whole-hearted life vision. Have your journal nearby.

- Make yourself comfortable.
- Close your eyes. Quiet your mind. Take five full, deep breaths.
- Connect with your inner wisdom and ask, "What is my Heartsong, my heart's desire, the best use of my unique talents and gifts?"
- Listen to the answer and pay attention to the images you see, the words you hear, and the sensations you experience.
- When you feel complete with the answer you've received, open your eyes and write it, draw it, or make a collage of it in your journal.
- Starting today, live it.

Each step of the way, when you get stumped and wonder, "How do I do this?", simply use the still small voice for guidance. Your work is to stay focused on what you want. Use your inner guidance to instruct you on what direction and actions to take.

Day 7: Write your reflections on your experience with listening to and following your still small voice.

> Behind every blade of grass is an angel whispering, "Grow."
>
> —THE TALMUD

WEEK 27

Use the Good Dishes

If I had my life to live over...

I would have burned the pink candle sculpted like a rose before it melted.

There would have been more "I love you's." More "I'm sorry's."

But mostly, given another shot at life, I would seize every minute...

Look at it and really see it...live it...and never give it back.

—ERMA BOMBECK,
FROM AN ESSAY SHE WROTE
AFTER BEING DIAGNOSED WITH CANCER

"Using the good dishes" is a metaphor for a powerful way to live your life more fully and happily. How many good dishes, special pieces of jewelry or clothing do you have put away for a special occasion? When you do use the good stuff, are you so anxious and worried that it might break or somehow get ruined that you really don't experience pleasure and joy when you do use it? How many special things do you keep under lock and key for safety?

One morning as I walked on the beach I wondered, "Does it take death to remind us of the sacredness of life? What if we lived our daily lives as a sacred act?" This is what "using the good dishes" is about: celebrating. So this week, "use the good dishes" and notice how you feel when you honor each moment.

From *Hannah's Gift: Lessons from a Life Fully Lived*
by Maria Housden

Today, Hannah (3 years old) was wearing her Christmas dress again, because, as she had explained to me, "This is a very, very special occasion." Nurse Katie was coming for tea.

Katie was one of Hannah's favorite nurses; she worked at the hospital where Hannah had her surgeries...

Now, Hannah was setting the tea party table herself. Walking slowly and carefully, she carried an eclectic assortment of china plates and cups, one at a time, from the kitchen to the coffee table in the living room. She ordered the cups and plates into a lopsided circle and set a white plastic daisy and vase from her Barbie tea set in the center. Three leftover birthday napkins, a Winnie-the-Pooh and two Little Mermaids, were joined by one that said "Happy New Year," lined up end to end "so we can see the pictures on them," Hannah explained.

As I watched Hannah arrange and rearrange the items on the table, I held myself back from making any suggestions. It wasn't easy. There was a part of me, I realized, that was overly critical of everything, that wanted to teach people, especially my children, about the "right" way to do things.

Hannah was smiling and humming, every once in a while stepping back to survey her work. She was in no hurry, and seemed completely unconcerned about the way a tea party is "supposed" to look. I watched her quietly, savoring the joy she was experiencing and the care she was giving to everything that she was doing. I longed to bring the same attention to the busyness in my everyday, to do something simply for the joy of doing it, without worrying whether people noticed or liked it.

* * *

How to Do It

Day 1: Use the good dishes today. Use them for breakfast in the morning and dinner at night. Set the table as though today is a special day—today *is* a special day because it is a day of your life. Use the crystal glasses or a special goblet that you love. Put a bouquet or a single flower on your table. Admire your good dishes and let them speak to you.

As I set the table with my good dishes, the ones my mother and father were given when they were married in 1947, I am filled with loving memories of my parents and special dinners. I used to worry that something would happen to them if I used them, and the truth is that something does happen—they evoke a sense of beauty, grace, and love that radiates from them, filling me and my home with those qualities.

Day 2: Wear a special item of clothing today. Whether it is the special nightgown you have been saving for "just the right time" or a piece of jewelry that you thought was too good to wear on an ordinary day, put it on, wear it, enjoy it.

Day 3: Wear something that says: "Life is a celebration, a precious gift." Wear those sunglasses with the rhinestones and the rose-colored lenses you bought on vacation many years ago and haven't worn since. Put on that lipstick that makes your lips sparkle, get the glitter out and sprinkle it on yourself. If you don't have anything like this stored away in your home, go out and buy something. Today is your day to play. Put a carnation in your lapel. There is no need to wait—today is your special day.

Day 4: Use the good soap, oil, and body lotion. Do you have a special way to pamper your body that you mean to do every day, and in the busyness of your daily routine you simply forget? Unwrap that special bar of soap you have been waiting to use. Or treat yourself to a new soap—a fragrance that you've wanted. Light candles in your bathroom. Take a bubble bath or a glorious shower. Use a body lotion that lets your body know, "I am grateful for my glorious body." Savor this experience with all your senses.

Day 5: Write a poem or an essay about "using the good dishes."

Day 6: Make a special meal and use the good dishes. This is a meal of only foods you love, maybe an old family favorite or that delicious treat from your favorite bakery. You love the way the food looks, smells, and tastes. Simply imagining eating this food makes your mouth water. Enjoy this loving nourishment.

Day 7: Reflect on and write your responses to the following questions:

- What did you learn by "using the good dishes"?
- How can you use this idea in your daily life?
- How do you feel when you celebrate each day as a precious present?

If I Had to Live My Life Over Again
by Nadine Stair

If I had to live my life over again, I'd dare to make more mistakes next time.

I'd relax. I would limber up. I'd be sillier than I have been this trip.

I would take fewer things seriously. I would take more chances. I would take more trips.

I would climb more mountains, swim more rivers.

I would eat more ice cream and less beans.

I would perhaps have more actual troubles, but I'd have fewer imaginary ones.

You see, I'm one of those people who live seriously and sanely hour after hour,

day after day.

Oh, I've had my moments, and if I had it to do over again, I'd have more of them.

In fact, I'd try to have nothing else, just moments, one after another, instead of living so many years ahead of each day.

I've been one of those persons who never goes anywhere without a thermometer,

a hot water bottle, a raincoat and a parachute.

If I had it to do again, I would travel lighter than I have.

If I had to live my life over, I would start barefoot earlier in the spring

and stay that way later in the fall.

I would go to more dances.

I would ride more merry-go-rounds.

I would pick more daisies.

WEEK 28

Exercise Your Body and Your Mind

> As a single footstep will not make a path on the earth, so a single thought will not make a pathway in the mind. To make a deep physical path, we walk again and again. To make a deep mental path, we must think over and over the kind of thoughts we wish to dominate our lives.
>
> —HENRY DAVID THOREAU

When you hear the word *exercise,* what automatically pops into your mind? If you are like most people, your response involves physical exercise. And while physical exercise clearly has an impact on your physical, emotional, mental, and spiritual health, brain-training exercise is also applicable for disciplining your mind and actually upgrading the software of your mind to align with your heart's desire.

Professional athletes repeatedly tell stories of the importance of training both their minds and their bodies. For example, Olympic skiers use the full resources of their imagination to create visualizations to practice their ski runs as preparation for actually skiing the slope. Exercising your mind, seeing yourself accomplishing the desired result, and seeing the muscles you are exercising are the foundation for excelling in your body when you participate in physical activity for fitness purposes. This is the power of the body-mind connection.

Exercise is a repeated action or discipline that strengthens a muscle, whether the muscles are your abdominals and lower back or your muscles of appreciation, forgiveness, and sense of humor. A crucial component in strengthening a muscle is regular practice, otherwise known as an exercise program. Often the greatest challenge to a regular practice is creating a new habit pattern. Humans follow the path of least resistance. This means that you follow the path of well-trod habits—brain pathways—in your thoughts, words, and actions. When you choose to make a change in your life, whether it is a regular physical exercise program, saying a prayer before each meal as an expression of appreciation, or listening to the still small voice within, you have to be disciplined to train your brain to upgrade the software of your mind that, when installed, creates new brain pathways that generate new thoughts, feelings, words, and actions. When you begin to feel seduced by the ease of the old habit, and you start to negotiate with thoughts like "I don't feel like going to the gym today; I'll go tomorrow and work out for twice as long" or "I don't feel like making a list of my accomplishments today, I promise to do it tomorrow," exercise your discipline and choose the new behavior.

How to Do It

Day 1: Create a physical exercise program to practice this week. If you already do physical exercise regularly, when you do it this week, pay particular attention to being present and awake as you do your exercises. When you are strengthening your triceps, feel your triceps. Pay attention to your breath, using your exhalations as you exert yourself and allowing yourself to renew and refresh with each inhalation. When I first began weight training, I looked forward to the time of rest between each set of ten or twelve reps. After many months of this focus, it occurred to me that I could rest on each inhalation, so I got to rest more frequently than I had when I was waiting to complete the reps. If you have not been exercising regularly, plan to do so this week. Even if you simply walk around the block three times this week, create an exercise plan and notice what you think and how you feel when you are doing it and when you complete it.

Day 2: Create a mental exercise program to practice this week. The purpose of this is for you to be more aware of what your thoughts are and to think thoughts that are supportive of you and your dreams. If you are someone who often complains about other drivers, or the weather, or not having enough time, then this week, exercise new thoughts about these topics.

Day 3: Stretch your body. Stretching increases your flexibility. If you are not sure of the appropriate form, go to a stretch class at your local gym or find a stretching video online. One that I like is the 5-Minute

Stretch Routine at http://www.youtube.com/watch?v=-iY5V0xiiKw. Be gentle with yourself, use your breath to deepen your stretch, and focus on the part of your body you are stretching as you do it. If you notice your mind wandering, bring your attention to your breath and your body. If you notice that you are holding your breath, release it and gently relax into the stretch. Let your body be your guide; listen to your body.

Day 4: Stretch your thoughts. Today, practice the idea that everything you and everyone else do is the best they can do at the moment. If they could have done something else, they would have. I have found that when I practice this exercise, I strengthen my muscle of acceptance of myself and others and I am living more wholeheartedly.

Day 5: Create a physical exercise program to practice this month. You may sign up for a class, join a gym, use your treadmill that has gotten dusty, or make plans with a friend to jog after work. On your calendar, schedule the days when you will exercise—and write it in the past tense, which is a mind game that generates the feeling of accomplishment even before you engage in the physical activity! During this month, do it.

Part of my exercise program is walking two miles at least four times a week. Some days I start my walk and I just don't want to do it. I hear a whiny self-talk voice giving reasons why I don't have to walk the full two miles today, but when I start putting one foot in front of the other, breathe in the fresh air, and notice how the sky looks, I begin to feel energized, and before I know it I am halfway done. I have learned that taking a few minutes to visualize having completed my exercise walk, and feeling a sense of accomplishment even before I take my first step, engages my mind and sets my body in motion. If there is a day when I am really not feeling well, I honor that. I use my body as my guide rather than listening to the whiny voice of habits that do not support my desired results.

Day 6: Exercise your mind today by spending two five-minute periods of time in silence, visualizing your desired results:

- Sit comfortably.
- Close your eyes.
- Gently focus on your breath, following the path of your inhalation and exhalation for five conscious breaths.
- Using the full resources of your imagination, create a scene of your dream fully accomplished, and then step into the scene.

Day 7: Reflect and write your response to the following questions:

- What did you learn about yourself?
- How can you incorporate exercise for your body and mind into your daily life?

WEEK 29

Use Your Feelings as Your Guide

Feelings are your personal guidance system.

Using your feelings as your guide is the most direct way to discover the impact of the thoughts you are thinking—whether or not you are conscious of your thoughts. Your feelings are a foolproof guidance system letting you know whether you are experiencing heaven or hell, love or fear, well-being or dis-ease. This does not mean that you are a good person if you have "positive" feelings and a bad person if you have "negative" feelings. The truth of who you are is always that you are an expression of God, Source Energy made manifest. You are made in the image of the Creator; simply because you forget that, it doesn't mean it is not true! Quantum physics has now scientifically demonstrated what ancient wisdom has taught through all time: We are energy. Another way of expressing this idea is that we are spiritual beings having a human experience.

Think of your body as an instrument. Just as musical instruments come in all sizes, shapes, and colors, so does our human instrument. All instruments have a wide range of sounds, some on-key and some off. It is the same with people. When your instrument is being played with the greatest ease and flow, you are vibrating at an energetic frequency of well-being and your sound is a joy to hear. Your feelings let you know when you are in tune or out of tune. When a musical instrument is out of tune, it is adjusted; while some time might be spent on the story of why the instrument is out of tune, the major focus is on the sound and returning to center—to being a finely tuned instrument. It seems as if human beings spend much more time on the story of why their instrument is out of tune than on simply doing a tune-up.

Have you noticed that when we ask each other how we are feeling, one usual response is a detailed explanation of what is going on in our lives—often a retelling of a story that is long over, drama, or tales of woe that may actually have been resolved? Since your experience is shaped by the thoughts you think, charged with emotional energy, the more you repeat, retell, and reactivate stories of woe, the more you use them as the seeds of your future and the fruits of your present. Another common response is to say that we are fine, when our inner experience is one of anxiety and dismay. In terms of the law of attraction, you attract according to your energetic vibration. If there is a discrepancy between your words and your vibration, vibration wins and is the attracting magnet.

You may be thinking, "Sure, this is easy to talk about, but my feelings are real." Precisely—your feelings are real. It is the meaning that you give to them, the stories that you tell and believe, that puts the cart before the horse. The cart is the story, and since you are a meaning-making machine, you make up your stories based on the patterns of thought and stories you have learned from your parents, teachers, and the collective consciousness of the planet. Your power as a meaning-making machine is that you can make up a new story in each and every moment.

Your feelings, which never lie, tell you your energetic frequency in the moment. When you are suffering, in hell, feeling anxious, frustrated, angry, impatient, hopeless, or helpless, your feelings—the sensations you feel in your body—are simply letting you know you are out of tune. Not whether you are good or bad or worthy or unworthy—these are human interpretations, stories you are making up! It is therefore very important to feel your feelings, whatever they are. Once you feel them—I repeat, *once you feel them*—use them as a reminder to tune your instrument. There is no need to judge yourself if you have what is called a "negative" feeling. It is simply a reminder that you are out of tune. "Positive" feelings are indicators that you are finely tuned. Simply put, you are either in flow with Source Energy (an instrument of love) or out of connection with Source Energy (off-key, off-center, out of tune). Which would you rather be? Use your feelings as your guide, make peace and happiness the point of view in the stories you create, and notice your Heartsong vibrating through you. Not only does this enhance your personal experience of well-being, it has a direct impact on your contribution to the collective consciousness of the world. So let your feelings be your guide.

How to Do It

Day 1: What sensations are you feeling in your body? Check in with yourself once an hour. Remember to focus on the physical sensations you are feeling, rather than the story about why you are feeling this particular feeling. Some examples of physical sensations are: "My breathing is full and deep, I have a smile on my face, I feel a slight tightness in my chest, there is a dull pain in the lower right side of my back." Today is the day to become aware of your body and your sensory experiences. Any time you notice tension in your body, breathe into that part of your body and allow the tension to be released as you exhale.

Day 2: Notice how you are feeling emotionally. Check in with yourself once an hour. Are you calm, content, joyful, overwhelmed, anxious, angry, or scared? What is the emotional name for the physical sensation you are experiencing? With an awareness of both the physical sensation and the emotion connected you strengthen your body mind connection.

Day 3: Allow your feelings to be your guide, and when you are off-center, out of tune, or experiencing hell, use the following technique:

- Acknowledge what you are feeling in the moment (*I am feeling frustrated and overwhelmed, with* sweaty palms and tightness in the center of my stomach).

- Choose what you would prefer to be feeling (*I choose to feel calm and focused, comfortable in my body*).
- For thirty seconds, use your imagination to focus on something that evokes the feeling you prefer to feel (*It's three o'clock in the afternoon. I am lounging on a comfortable beach chair on the beach in East Hampton. I am watching the gentle flow of the waves, feeling the sun-drenched breeze on my body.*). It is usually easier to imagine a scene that is unrelated to the content of what is causing your agitation. The purpose of this exercise is to develop your ability to change your vibration at the point of your greatest power—*now.*
- Continue on with your life (cooking dinner, paying your bills, taking a bath, driving to work, and so forth).

Day 4: Allow your feelings to be your guide, and when you are off-center, out of tune, or experiencing hell, use the following technique:

- Acknowledge what you are feeling in the moment, including both the emotional name for the feeling (angry, frustrated) and the sensations in your body (tension in my temples, a frown on my face, heart pounding in my chest).
- Choose what you would prefer to be feeling (calm, heart beating gently, a smile on my face, at ease, confident).

- Ask yourself what you are believing about the current situation that is creating the feeling you are having (*I am afraid that I'm not going to get to my job interview on time, and I will screw up getting this new job before I even get there; I believe that I am helpless in dealing with my health problems; I believe I am never going to be in a satisfying relationship;* and so forth).
- Make up a belief that supports the way you want to feel, and focus your attention on your new belief *(I have an interview for a great job, I deserve to have the job of my dreams; I have support and excellent care in experiencing well-being in my life; I am in a loving marriage).*
- Continue with your day.

Day 5: During the day, whenever you notice that you are feeling like a victim, make up a new story about the circumstances you are in. Imagine a story in which you are a finely tuned instrument and everything is perfect the way it is. I was recently feeling like a victim and plotting revenge about something going on in my home. I noticed that I had a desire to tell others of the drama. So I vented to a friend, who did not get seduced by the story, and once I did that, I remembered that continued focus on the story was simply that, continued focus on the story. I asked myself, "What would Love do here?" I kept being pulled back in my mind to the drama, and I kept asking "What would Love do here?" Within moments I felt calmer and thought, "We all did the best we could do."

Later on, as I was sitting quietly, I had memories of similar circumstances in my life. I was tempted to use them to get back into the drama. Instead I asked

"What would Love do here?" and I followed the advice I heard from my still small voice within. I was loving, in the tone of my voice, in my thoughts. Within hours I had moved through this experience and had also let go of past baggage. I let my feelings be my guide, and when my feelings indicated that I was off-key, I did a tune-up. I needed many tune-ups during those hours, so I got them! During the next two days, I was repeatedly tempted to tell the story about what had happened and what I had learned. I knew that the temptation was more about habit than anything else and that there was no need to tell the story, only to express my love.

Day 6: Create your own set of procedures for you to use when your feelings are telling you that you need a tune-up. What are some operating instructions you can follow? Put these instructions in place where you can see them and use them. Every time you use them, give yourself a pat on the back. Know that you are creating a new pattern, one that includes regular check-ups and maintenance to keep your instrument finely tuned. Update your operating instructions as necessary.

Day 7: Reflect and write your response to the following questions:

- What did you learn when you used your feelings as your GPS?
- How can you use what you learned so that being loving, kind, and compassionate is the dominant tune you sing?

WEEK 30

Read Inspiring Words

Quotes influence and move us. Once we hear those words and feel the impact, they forever help shape our thinking. Words are the language of the mind; we do not give enough importance to their ability to hurt or heal.

—DAVID BROMFIELD

Reading inspiring words is a powerful way to focus your attention. Wholehearted living begins as all experiences begin, with a thought charged with an energetic vibration/frequency (energy in motion = e-motion = emotion). Therefore inspiring words, in the form of a single word, a phrase, poetry, essays, and stories, have the power to focus our attention in the moment, awakening and reinforcing our well-being.

Words and sounds are magic with the power to transform your experience—to soothe a broken heart, put a smile on your face, offer a new view of a situation, and evoke the sacred that is always alive in the precious present. Read inspiring words aloud this week; feel each word resonate within your being. As you read, if your attention wanders, go back to the beginning of what you are reading with the intent of being in communion (common union) with the words, allowing them to illuminate your way and your day.

How to Do It

Begin and end each day this week with an inspirational reading. This may be a continuation of readings from a book of daily readings that you already read regularly, or you may choose a particular poet to read each morning, or scan the books in your home and notice which one *feels* just right for this assignment. Focus your full attention on your reading; put down your coffee cup and clear your mind of everything but the present moment and the gifts of inspiration in the words you are reading aloud. I often do this reading in bed, upon waking up and before going to sleep (Mark Nepo is my go-to poet each morning as I write this book). If you have an altar in your home, or a special room or chair, you may want to do your reading there.

Some books of daily readings that have inspired me are:

- *The Courage to Change* by Al-Anon Family Groups
- *Daring Greatly* by Brene Brown
- *Imperfect Spirituality* by Polly Campbell
- *The Promise of a New Day* by Karen Casey and Martha Vanceburg
- *The Seven Spiritual Laws of Success* by Deepak Chopra

- *Night Light: A Book of Nighttime Meditations* by Amy E. Dean
- *A Course in Miracles* by The Foundation for Inner Peace
- *It's Never Too Late to Be What You Might Have Been* by BJ Gallagher
- *The Grateful Table* by Brenda Knight
- *Living Life as a Thank You* by Nina Lesowitz and Mary Beth Sammons
- *What Are You Waiting For?* by Kristen Moeller
- *Reduced to Joy* by Mark Nepo
- *The Inspired Life* by Susyn Reeve

Day 1: Search the web for inspiring quotations. Choose a few to write down and post them where they will capture your attention (on your screen saver, in your appointment book, on your bathroom mirror, on your dashboard, on your closet door, on your bedside table, etc.). When you see them, stop what you are doing for a moment, read the inspiring words, and invite each word to fill your being.

Day 2: Read the *Prayer for Wholehearted Living* on page xxx once an hour. Embody the words. At the end of the day, write the impact of this focus in your journal.

Day 3: Go to your local library or bookstore, or just to a bookshelf (yours or a friend's). Choose a book with words of inspiration to read and begin reading it. If you are like me, you may have books in your personal library that you bought and have never opened—this may be the time to open one of them.

Day 4: Begin an inspiration journal or Pinterest board. Today, begin writing, designing, or pinning quotes, adding to it whenever you come across something that captures your attention and speaks to you—whether it ignites chills, giggles, or tears. I have found that the act of writing and saying the words aloud as I form them seems to amplify my experience. Experiment.

Day 5: Write your own words of inspiration. This may be a poem or a response to any or all of the following questions:

- The key to wholehearted living is _____.
- The greatest life lesson is _____.
- The most important words of wisdom I want to share with the children in my life are _____ _____.

Day 6: Choose words that inspire you and share them with three people, as well as with your friends on Facebook or any other social media sites you frequent.

Day 7: Reflect and write your response to the following questions:

- How did reading inspiring words impact your day?
- If this is a new practice for you, do you want to continue it daily?
- Is there a particular prayer or quotation that you want to focus on regularly as a way to direct your attention when you are stressed and off-center?

Come, whoever you are! Wanderer,
worshipper, Lover of Leaving

Come. This is not a caravan of despair.
It doesn't matter if you've broken

your vow a thousand times, still

Come, and yet again
Come!

—RUMI

WEEK 31
Take a Risk

And then the day came when the risk to remain tight in the bud was more painful than the risk it took to blossom.

—ANAÏS NIN

Taking a risk is a way to step outside of everyday habits and consciously make choices that echo your Heartsong. Taking a risk is doing something in a different way, whether it is changing your thinking or changing a habitual action. It often opens the way to new possibilities and ultimately to greater peace and happiness. Sometimes taking a risk means speaking up and voicing your point of view; other times, it's a risk to remain silent and listen. It may be a risk to start a new business, to talk with your boss about a raise, to enroll in a class, to try out for a part with your local theater group. It may be a risk to share your love with a loved one, or to go to the gym even though you don't remember when you last exercised. It may be a risk to get a new haircut, or to wear the clothes you have only tried on in the privacy of your room. It may be a risk to go on a trip by yourself, or to ask for help.

Life is filled with opportunities to be fully alive, to live your heart's desire. It is up to you to take the action, to take the risk and feel the personal freedom you can have access to when you say "Yes." So this week, take a risk, and if you experience fear or feel paralyzed, take a deep breath and do it anyway. Keep in mind that this is not about being a daredevil. This is about listening to the message of your heart and responding with a resounding *Yes*.

How to Do It

Day 1: In the words of Robert Frost, "Two roads diverged in a wood, and I—I took the one less traveled by, And that has made all the difference." Take the road less traveled today. Take a risk. Get a new haircut. Say "I love you" aloud. Sign up at the gym. Find out about that investment you have been wondering about. Enroll in the improv workshop that you've daydreamed about.

Day 2: Risk dreaming your big dream. Write down your heart's desire. If you knew that success was guaranteed and that all the resources of the universe were available to you, what would you dare to dream? Would you be in a leading role on Broadway, or traveling the world, or working as a physician, or at home when your kids arrive from school each day, or turning your grandmother's apple pie recipe into a successful business and donating a portion of the profits to a cause you love? This is the dream you'll write down today. Go for it. Dream big. Start writing with the following sentences: *Today I am fully living my heart's desire, my big dream. I am:*

Day 3: Take a step toward living your big dream today.

Day 4: Create a virtual reality of your big dream and visualize it for sixty seconds, three times a day (today and every day). See yourself in your life living your dream. Use the full resources of your imagination as you live the virtual reality of your heart's desire. Be specific about where you are, what you are wearing, the sounds you hear, the tastes and fragrances of your heart's desire, how you are feeling. Make sure to put yourself into the scene.

Day 5: Risk expressing your love today. Allow every thought you think, every word you say, and every action you take to be an expression of love. If, by habit, you make a slip, simply ask yourself, "What would love do here?" and listen to the answer, and get back on track.

Day 6: Every time you get a nudge today to perform an act of kindness, act on it. If there is someone on the street asking you for money and you are inclined to give, but then wonder if she will simply use the money for a drink, give anyway. If you see some trash on the street and are inclined to pick it up, bend down and pick it up. If it seems as if the person in front of you at the supermarket needs some help with their packages, offer to help.

Day 7: Write a poem about your experience of taking risks. Reflect and write your responses to the following questions:

- How does taking risks enhance your experience of living wholeheartedly?
- How can you incorporate this point of view into your life so that you risk expressing your love to yourself and those around you, every day?

Taking a Risk

In a psychology class I took in college, the professor gave us an assessment to determine if we were risk takers. I got a very high score and was happy to know that I was a risk taker. And while my life has been filled with many risks, as I wrote this chapter, one particular risk kept coming to mind. I was invited to participate in a special gathering of Mount Sinai Medical Center and New York University Medical Center employees on September 14, 2001. The purpose of this gathering was to offer support to New Yorkers experiencing the shock of September 11. While these medical centers had been my clients for many years, this time I was invited to participate in my role of interfaith minister—I had been ordained earlier, in June. I was honored and humbled by this invitation, and since Manhattan is where I was born and raised, it had special meaning for me. I gave a lot of thought to what I was going to say. On the two-hour bus ride into the city from my home in East Hampton, I questioned whether I had the courage to end my words with a version of the Loving Kindness Prayer:

May I be at peace.
May my heart remain open.
May I awaken to the Light
of my own true nature.
May I be healed.
May I be a source of healing
for all beings.

May you be at peace.
May your heart remain open.
May you awaken to the Light
of your own true nature.
May you be healed.
May you be a source of healing
for all beings.

May my enemies be at peace.
May my enemies' hearts remain open.
May my enemies awaken to the Light
of their own true nature.
May my enemies be healed.
May my enemies be a source of healing
for all beings.

I didn't want to offend people by asking that they include enemies in this prayer, yet in the very core of my being, these felt like the most healing words I could offer and be true to myself. I took the risk. At the end of the gathering, some people approached me and said they could never forgive their enemies, and others thanked me. I knew then that being true to myself without judging the reactions of others was a risk worth taking.

WEEK 32
Ask for Help

Ask, and it shall be given you;
seek, and ye shall find;
knock, and it shall be opened unto you.

— MATTHEW 7:7

Asking for help and receiving support are necessary habits for wholehearted living. Most people have difficulty establishing this habit pattern. Do you? Do you prefer to help others, and dislike asking for help? Are you attached to an idea that you will have a higher score on your permanent record (where is this permanent record, anyway?) if you do it yourself? Are you someone who does not want to bother others or be indebted to them? Do you think that your request for help will be a burden to the person you are thinking of asking—and then, when you don't ask for help, you wonder why people don't help you the way you help them? Perhaps then you even get angry at yourself, or at the person who you never asked for help!

The flow of Love—from our hearts and into our hearts—requires both giving and receiving, asking and allowing. Help, resources, abundance, and miracles are available to you simply by asking, wrapped in faith (believing in something) and allowing yourself to receive. This is true in all areas of your life, whether it is asking for help carrying heavy packages, stopping at a gas station to ask for directions, asking a friend for a shoulder to cry on, asking a credit card company for a new payment plan, or asking God to guide you through a dark night of the soul. The more you ask, the more you receive, the more connected and supported you feel, and the more you have to offer.

We cannot climb up a rope that is attached only to our own belt.
—WILLIAM EARNEST HOCKING

How to Do It

Day 1: Make a list of the kinds of help you'd like to receive—e.g. carrying packages, keeping the house in order, a shoulder to cry on, a hug, a new perspective for a stressful situation. Be creative. Identify who you might ask for each type of help.

Day 2: Just do it. When you need help, ask for it. If the person you ask is unable to help you, remember, this does not mean you should not have asked and that no one wants to help you. It simply means that that person was not available to help you. So ask someone else.

Day 3: Acknowledge yourself when you ask for help: *Good for me, I asked for help.* This will help to create a new pattern, making it easier for you to continue to ask for help.

Day 4: When you ask for help and it is given to you, receive it. Simply say, "Thank you." You do not owe the person who helped you. In a true helping relationship, both the receiver and the giver benefit.

Day 5: Help someone and notice how good you feel for having been helpful. Remember this when you ask someone to help you; you are giving them the opportunity to have that good feeling.

Day 6: Write an essay, poem, or words of wisdom about your experience asking for help.

Day 7: Reflect on and write your response to the following questions:

- What did you learn by asking for help?
- What blocked the flow of asking and receiving?
- What made it easier for you to ask for help?
- What is the most important lesson you learned about asking for and allowing help?

Information Please

Author unknown

When I was quite young, my father had one of the first telephones in our neighborhood. I remember the well-polished, old case fastened to the wall. The shiny receiver hung on the side of the box. I was too little to reach the telephone, but used to listen with fascination when my mother used to talk to it. Then I discovered that somewhere inside the wonderful device lived an amazing person—her name was *Information Please* and there was nothing she did not know. *Information Please* could supply anybody's number and the correct time.

My first personal experience with this genie-in-the-bottle came one day while my mother was visiting a neighbor. Amusing myself at the tool bench in the basement, I whacked my finger with a hammer. The pain was terrible, but there didn't seem to be any reason to keep crying because there was no one home to give sympathy. I walked around the house sucking my throbbing finger, finally arriving at the stairway. The telephone! Quickly, I ran for the footstool in the parlor and dragged it to the landing. Climbing up, I unhooked the receiver and held it to my ear.

"Information Please," I said into the mouthpiece just above my head. A click or two and a small clear voice spoke into my ear.

"Information."

"I hurt my finger..." I wailed into the phone. The tears came readily enough now that I had an audience.

"Isn't your mother home?" came the question.

"Nobody's home but me," I blubbered.

"Are you bleeding?" the voice asked.

"No," I replied. "I hit my finger with the hammer and it hurts."

"Can you open the icebox?" she asked. I said I could.

"Then chip off a little piece of ice and hold it to your finger," said the voice.

After that, I called *Information Please* for everything. I asked her for help with my geography homework and she told me where Philadelphia was. She helped me with my math. She told me my pet chipmunk that I had caught in the park the day before would eat fruit and nuts. Then, there was the time Petey, our pet canary, died. I called *Information Please* and told her the sad story. She listened, and then said the usual things grown-ups say to soothe a child. But I was not consoled. I asked her, "Why is it that birds should sing so beautifully and bring joy to all families, only to end up as a heap of feathers on the bottom of a cage?" She must have sensed my deep concern, for she said quietly, "Paul, always remember that there are other worlds to sing in."

Somehow I felt better. Another day I was on the telephone. "Information Please."

"Information," said the now familiar voice.

"How do you spell *fix*?" I asked.

All this took place in a small town in the Pacific Northwest.

When I was nine years old, we moved across the country to Boston. I missed my friend very much. *Information Please* belonged in that old wooden box back home and I somehow never thought of trying the shiny new phone that sat on the table in the hall. As I grew into my teens, the memories of those childhood conversations never really left me. Often, in moments of doubt and perplexity, I would recall the serene sense of security I had then. I appreciated now how patient, understanding, and kind she was to have spent her time on a little boy.

A few years later, on my way west to college, my plane put down in Seattle. I had about half an hour between planes. I spent fifteen minutes on the phone with my sister, who lived there now. Then, without thinking what I was doing, I dialed my hometown operator and said, "Information Please." Miraculously I heard a small, clear voice I knew so well say, "Information." I hadn't planned this, but I heard myself saying, "Could you please tell me how to spell *fix?*"

There was a long pause, then the soft spoken answer, "I guess your finger must have healed by now."

I laughed. "So it's really still you," I said. "I wonder if you have any idea how much you meant to me during that time."

"I wonder," she said, "if you know how much your calls meant to me. I never had any children and I used to look forward to your calls."

I told her how often I had thought of her over the years, and I asked if I could call her again when I came back to visit my sister.

"Please do," she said. "Just ask for Sally."

Three months later I was back in Seattle. A different voice answered, "Information." I asked for Sally. "Are you a friend?" she said.

"Yes, a very old friend," I answered.

"I'm sorry to have to tell you this," she said. "Sally

had been working part time for the past few years because she was sick. She died five weeks ago."

Before I could hang up she said, "Wait a minute. Did you say your name was Paul?"

"Yes."

"Well, Sally left a message for you. She wrote it down in case you called. Let me read it to you." The note said, "Tell him I still say there are other worlds to sing in. He'll know what I mean."

WEEK 33

Be Forgiving

Forgiveness is the answer to the child's dream of a miracle by which what is broken is made whole again, what is soiled is made clean.

—DAG HAMMARSKJÖLD

Forgiveness is a shift in consciousness and perception that opens up a space in your heart where you are imprisoned by guilt, blame, shame, anger, and regret. Whether you are forgiving yourself, another person, a group, or an institution, the forgiver receives the greatest gift.

An interesting thing about human beings is that we seem to be the only species that continually punishes ourselves by re-living, in our minds, situations from the past. Whether you regret something you have said or done or blame someone else for what they have done to you, each time you remember the situation, you reactivate the feelings of hurt, pain, anger, and sadness.

Forgiveness is the action that releases and frees you from past pain, opening your heart and mind to love.

How to Do It

Day 1: Make a Forgiveness List. A Forgiveness List includes the people you are forgiving and what you are forgiving them for. The format for the items on your list is: *I forgive* (name of person) *for* (what you are forgiving them for).

Be aware that as you write this list, you may not actually feel ready to fully forgive; this is okay. This is an opportunity to start the process, to give energy to the idea of being forgiving, and to notice which items on your list will need more attention to forgive. You will know when you have forgiven and are complete with an item on your list when you no longer feel a negative emotional charge when that person pops into your mind. Rather, you feel a lightness in your being, you have more energy. You may even feel gratitude, connection, and love for the worthy opponent who gave you the opportunity to hone your forgiveness muscle. Remember, forgiveness is not about condoning someone's behavior; rather, it is accepting that the person you are forgiving (even if it's yourself) was doing the very best they could, based on their thinking—their programming—at the time of the incident you are forgiving.

Items on your forgiveness list may include the following:

- I forgive myself for yelling at my kids this morning.
- I forgive myself for complaining to my friends about my husband.

- I forgive myself for hating myself for being over-weight.
- I forgive my girlfriend for always being late.
- I forgive my sister for not sending me a birthday card.
- I forgive my boss for never saying "Thank you."
- I forgive my partner for having an affair.
- I forgive the politicians whose positions I disagree with.
- I forgive terrorists for not knowing that we are all connected and that our true enemies are hatred and fear.
- I forgive my father for his alcoholism.
- I forgive Mrs. Smith, my art teacher in elementary school, for telling me, in front of the whole class, that my drawing was the worst in the class.

Day 2: Write a forgiveness letter to yourself. This is a genuine, loving letter from you to you, in which you forgive yourself for all of the things you have been blaming yourself for, all of the things you regret and feel guilty about, all of the abusive thoughts you have had about yourself that you *thought* were true. Use the items on your forgiveness list as a place to start; others may pop up once you begin writing. As you write this letter, you may reactivate some old hurt feelings. Allow yourself to feel them and continue to forgive yourself for the abusive beliefs and actions you directed toward yourself.

Write whatever pops into your mind; this letter is for your eyes only. As you are impeccable with your words and honest with what you are feeling, you will move through these old stories about yourself that blocked the flow of love in your life. Once your letter is complete, read it aloud to yourself until you feel the energy of forgiveness moving through your being—this may take more than one reading, more than one day.

Day 3: Write a forgiveness letter to someone else on your list, and then write the response you'd like to receive from them. As you do this, your perception of them will change, and you will see the circumstance that had been the cause of so much pain for you in a different light. Read your letter aloud, burn it, and use the ashes as fertilizer for a plant, knowing that you are nurturing new possibilities in your relationship with the person you are forgiving. (This letter can be written to a person who has passed on as well as one who is alive.)

Day 4: Write in your journal about forgiveness. What does it mean to you? What have you learned from focusing on it? What blocks you from forgiving? What do Jesus' words from the cross, "Father, forgive them, for they do not know what they do," mean to you? How can you use his lesson in your life?

Day 5: Choose someone from your list and visualize or imagine a forgiveness conversation with them. You may want to record the following visualization and use it during this exercise:

- Sitting in a chair, make yourself comfortable. With your feet on the floor and your hands resting gently on your thighs, close your eyes and focus on your breath, breathing in calm and relaxation and exhaling into a sigh of comfort.

- Using the full resources of your imagination, see yourself in a special sacred space. This may be a place you have actually been or simply a creation of your imagination. Notice how your sacred space looks. Where is it? What's in it? What colors do you see? With a clear sense of your sacred space filling your being, step into your sacred place and make yourself comfortable. Sit down, feeling comfortable and supported.

- Set your intention for this exercise by repeating, in your mind, the following words: "In order to let go of blocks to the flow of love in my life, I am ready and willing to forgive. I know that through the act of forgiveness I free myself from the past and open my heart and mind to love, compassion, and kindness. Forgiveness is a gift I give myself. I am now ready to forgive (the name of the person you wish to forgive)."

- Seeing this person in your mind, tell him/her what you forgive them for.
    o "I forgive you for _____."
       (If you experience anger, sadness, hurt, or emotional pain, allow yourself to feel it, express it, and continue.)
    o "I wish you had _____."
    o "I now know that your words and actions were the best you could do at the time, and I forgive you." (Leave time on the tape for you to complete this part of the exercise.)

- Take a deep breath, relaxing your focus and keeping your eyes closed. Feel a sense of calm and renewal filling your being. Know that your sacred place is always available for you—a safe and loving place to forgive.

Day 6: Have a forgiveness conversation. Talk with someone on your list who you have forgiven in your heart, over the phone or in person. Depending on the situation, the conversation may be a simple "I've missed you and am sorry that we had a misunderstanding," or it may focus more on the circumstances—not to rehash it and "be right," but rather to clear the air and move on.

Day 7: Acknowledge yourself for the powerful steps you have taken to open yourself to live a wholehearted life. Write what you have learned in your journal and read over your forgiveness list, crossing off those names that no longer belong on the list. Commit to having the next forty days be a time of practicing forgiveness—setting in motion a new habit for life.

> When I have forgiven myself and remembered who I Am, I will bless everyone and everything I see.
>
> —A COURSE IN MIRACLES

What Are You Really Forgiving?

One day, just before the holidays in 1985, I had an experience of forgiveness that transformed my understanding of forgiveness and transformed my life. Byll and I had been divorced for six years when I wrote to him asking for copies of some home movies we had made during our marriage. My boyfriend was curious to get a glimpse of another time of my life, and I was also eager to see the movies of my dad, who had died eleven years earlier. Byll responded that he had considered my request and decided he did not want to send me the movies. I was shocked, particularly since some of the movies were of my dad and Byll was the director of a hospice program!

I assumed he had decided not to send them to me because I had not included money to make copies of the films. So I wrote to him, enclosed a check, and made sure to point out (with an attitude) that since he was a hospice director, he *should* understand that I wanted to see the home movies of my dad.

Byll's next letter echoed the sentiments of the first: "I made movies before I met you and I've continued to make movies since we've been divorced, and I will decide who gets to see my movies." I thought, "This guy has a problem!"

Months passed. A friend invited me to a presentation on forgiveness at The Open Center in New York City. We sat listening as Robin Casajarian spoke about the power of forgiveness. She led us through a guided visualization. I closed my eyes and concentrated on her words. "See a door on the right-hand side of the room," she said. "In a few moments, someone will walk through that door. Forgive that person." The door opened and Byll walked to the center of the room and stood directly in front of me.

My ego was ready to forgive with no strings attached— to let go—and I said, "I forgive you for having affairs and for being unavailable during the time when my father was dying." Then I heard another voice, quieter this time, but concise and direct, as though it came straight from my heart: "I forgive you for loving me."

I was stunned.

I knew that this was the profound truth beneath all the obvious reasons I had been angry with him during our marriage. In order for me to have accepted his love, I had to first love myself, and I *didn't* love myself. Through the years of our marriage, I had projected all the self-loathing I felt for myself onto him. The more he loved me, the more I projected. With this realization, I felt energized, light-hearted, and free, and I knew that a very important lesson had been revealed to me.

Ten days later I was in New Hampshire (where Byll and I had once lived together and he now lived) for the holidays. On New Year's Eve, I was in a giant super-market, and as I walked through the store I suddenly knew that Byll was there as well. I walked straight to where he was! We said hello and then he asked, "Did you get the movies I sent to you about ten days ago?"

As soon as I truly forgave Byll for loving me and ultimately forgave myself for believing that I was not worthy of love, the home movies that contained the loving memories of our life together were on their way to me.

This is the way forgiveness works. When we finally let go of the hurt, the anger, the need to be right, and the need to make others wrong, we not only release ourselves from the bonds of resentment, we discover that the wonderful things in life find their way to us— and that LOVE illuminates the path.

Forgiveness

Author unknown

To forgive, is not to forget.
To forgive is really to remember:
That nobody is perfect
That each of us stumbles when we want so much to stay
    upright.
That each of us says things we wish we had not said.
That we can all forget that Love is more important than
    being right.

To forgive is really to remember:
That we are so much more than our mistakes.
That we are often more kind and caring.
That accepting another's flaws can help us accept our
    own.

To forgive is to remember:
That the odds are pretty good that we might soon need
    to be forgiven ourselves.
That life sometimes gives us more than we can handle
    gracefully.

To forgive is to remember:
That we have room in our heart to
Begin again
And again
and again and again.

WEEK 34

Spend Time with a Pet

There is no psychiatrist in the world like a puppy licking
your face.

—BEN WILLIAMS

Spending time with a pet is a source of joy, pleasure,
and amusement. As I write, my sheepdog, Rosie, is
asleep beside my desk chair. When she wakes up, she
nuzzles up to me. I pet her and chat with her, and then
she usually finds another spot to take a nap, unless a
bone or something outside captures her attention. I am
her main "sheep"! She keeps an eye on me, and that
is quite literal, since she is blind in one eye. My cat
Lucy is out and about. I've been told by neighbors that
she stops by their homes and visits, as she knows her
way around the neighborhood. She loves sleeping on
the corner of the living room couch during the day and

at the foot of my bed at night, and walking across my desk and adding a few letters to my manuscript when the keyboard is in her path. She is a great stalker. She has taught me about patience and focus. I am joyously grateful for having these beings in my life. Rosie reminds me daily to greet each day with enthusiasm, eat when I'm hungry, sleep when I'm tired, and always be ready for an adventure when I go outside, and that hugging is always acceptable.

Did you realize that Dog is God spelled back-wards?
So, if a Dog is your mirror, you are seeing God!

Pets allow for cross-species communion, and sometimes that is the best remedy for the noise and chatter that fills our minds. Whether you are mesmerized by the activity in a fish tank, in awe of the underwater world when snorkeling, fascinated by a TV nature program, delighted when swimming with dolphins, inspired by a heroic act of a four-legged creature in a movie, surprised by the articulate words of a parrot, or soothed by the cuddly softness of your favorite stuffed animal, spending time with a pet is a prescription for peace and happiness.

How to Do It

Day 1: Honor the fauna you share your space with: the flies, the birds, the dogs, the cats. What do you see in the course of your daily life? This may mean that you have to stop yourself from swatting some winged insects as they fly toward you.

I used to be afraid of insects, and the thought of a cockroach gave me the creeps. In 1978, as I was preparing to move back to New York City, one of my biggest concerns was that there would be cockroaches in my apartment, no matter how clean it was. A few months before my move, I went to a workshop that was given by Dorothy MacLean, one of the founders of the Findhorn Community. She talked about every being—plants, insects, birds, animals, trees, flowers, rocks—actually everything—having consciousness, and that it was possible to communicate, consciousness to consciousness. I decided I would communicate with cockroach consciousness. I was willing to make a deal. It went like this: "I won't kill you as long as you stay out of sight when I'm around. It's okay for you to be in my apartment, I just don't want to see you. When you hear me coming, scat." It worked. In the nine years I lived there, I saw cockroaches about five times. When I saw them, I didn't kill them. Instead, I reminded them of our agreement.

Today, become aware of the amazing beings that coexist with you. If there are some that are scary to you, begin to change your thinking about them and make a deal!

Day 2: Spend time with a pet or an animal today. If you have a dog, when you walk him, actually be with him, rather than going on a walk on automatic. Act as if you are spending time with a good friend. If you don't have a pet, you might stop by a local zoo or aquarium and spend time connecting with the beings there. You might stop by your local pet shelter and see about volunteering to spend time with the animals there.

Day 3: Watch a movie where animals have leading roles.

Day 4: Talk with three people about their pets. Ask:

- What is special about your pet?
- Why do you have that particular pet?
- How does your pet contribute to your being open-hearted and loving?

Day 5: Play with acting as if you are an animal. Give yourself some space. Start out lying on the floor with your eyes closed and imagine that you are a cat. Stretch into those long, graceful cat stretches. When another animal pops into your mind, be that animal. You might find it quite enjoyable to waddle around your living room like a penguin! Allow your imagination to be your guide. Do this for at least fifteen minutes and notice how you feel afterward.

Day 6: Spend time with a pet again today—your own or a friend's—or visit the seagulls down near the water, or the birds in a nearby park. Allow your mind to focus on communing with this being, and notice what happens when you focus your attention on being with a pet.

Day 7: Reflect and write your response to the following questions:

- What did you notice about yourself when you spent time with a pet or animal?
- What did you learn?
- How do you feel when you open your heart and mind to being with an animal?
- How does being with a pet contribute to your peace of mind?

*From the oyster to the eagle, from the swine to the
    tiger,
all animals are to be found in men and each of them
exists in some man, sometimes several at the time.
Animals are nothing but the portrayal of our virtues
and vices made manifest to our eyes, the visible
reflections of our souls. God displays them
to us to give us food for thought.*

—VICTOR HUGO, *LES MISERABLES*

WEEK 35

Seize the Moment—
Be Here Now

Realize that now, in this moment of time, you are creating. You are creating your next moment. That is what's real.

—SARA PADDISON

Seizing the moment, being here now, is the access point to the greatest power, the most potent creative energy in our lives. The present moment is all that we ever really have. Unfortunately, we often mask the present moment in thoughts and worries about the past or future. We re-live past hurts, over and over and over again. Like the tagline I heard many years ago on the History Channel, we bring the past to life. Or we spend time imagining the past repeating itself in our future, thereby using the law of attraction to attract to ourselves more of the same, giving much credence to the idea of history repeating itself! Indeed, we recreate history through where we focus our attention.

I am amazed by our masterful ability to have our body be in one place and our mind be somewhere else. It may even be happening to you right now, as you are reading this. Your mind may be wandering, and you have to consciously choose to bring your attention back to this page, now.

When you seize the moment, you experience the wonder and mystery that are always present in our world.

Early one April it was unseasonably hot for three days. The temperature was in the nineties, and the heat was intensified because most of the leaves on the trees were still tight in the bud. I packed up my beach chair, laptop, and dog and went to the beach to write. Rather than writing, I began to focus on the heat gently caressing my skin, the sound of the surf, and the children laughing at the water's edge. I watched my dog running easily and gracefully with other dogs. Everything I looked at, everything I heard and experienced, was sparkling with life. This unexpected April heat seemed to be an alarm clock that woke me up to my daily life. During the next two days I noticed flowers blooming within hours, leaves opening on the trees, birds flying and singing. I felt as though I actually lived in a Disney movie. Yellow, purple, and pink flowers. Leaves all shades of green. Birds with red bellies, blue, and hints of yellow flying in my yard, on my lane. I thought, "I really do live in a fairy tale." Since that day, my awareness of my surroundings has been reawakened. My ability to direct my attention to the beauty, mystery, and power of the present moment is as simple as focusing my attention on my surroundings.

I am also aware that it is possible to focus on the

present moment and see litter on the street, hear the noise of honking horns, see homeless people in need, and feel overwhelmed and frustrated. But does it really help anyone to wallow in those thoughts? So if you notice that your present moment is filled with thoughts of what is wrong and feelings of unhappiness, do something about it. Pick up the litter that you see; imagine the sounds of the car horns as music; hear them mingle with the whoosh of the breeze, the song of the birds, and the jet engine above. Give the homeless person a sandwich, a smile, some loose change, or a prayer for her well-being.

One day while I was standing on a street corner waiting for the red light to turn green, I overheard a well-dressed, wealthy-looking man having a conversation with a man standing on the street corner, poorly dressed and asking for money. The man in the suit was talking with the other man about Eckhart Tolle's book *The Power of Now* and how it helped him change his life. I smiled, grateful that this conversation was reminding me of the richness of now.

I have always felt such a sense of grace when I pass a homeless person who says "God bless you" to me, whether or not I have given anything. It is at times like this that I become supremely aware that no matter what the circumstance, we always have a present to give in the moment.

You create your experience by where you place your attention. Your future first lives in your thoughts, in your imagination, in the present. Honor your today and nourish the seeds of a bountiful future by honoring, embracing, and rejoicing in this moment, the precious present.

How to Do It

Day 1: Once an hour, bring your attention to the present moment. Do it by focusing on your sensory experience. For instance, I am sitting on my desk chair, and my right ankle is resting on my left thigh. My left foot is on the base of my desk chair. I am looking at my computer screen. My fingers are gently tapping against the keys on my black computer keyboard. With each keystroke I hear a tapping sound. My back is supported by the back of the chair. I hear the hum of the swimming pool filter in the background. I have a smile on my face.

Day 2: Every time you notice your mind wandering, bring your focus to the present moment by consciously focusing your attention on your breath or your sensory experience. For example, as you relive the argument you had with your girlfriend yesterday, bring your attention to the present moment. As you imagine the rush hour traffic later this evening, bring your attention to the present moment. As you plot revenge against your boss who has once again given you a last-minute project to complete, bring your attention to the present moment. It doesn't matter what storyline you are following in your mind. Even if you are imagining a great night of romance, for the sake of this practice, strengthen your ability to consciously focus your attention on the present moment.

Day 3: Meditate for ten to twenty minutes in the morning and ten to twenty minutes in the evening.

- Sit comfortably.
- Close your eyes.
- Focus your attention on your breath.
- Inhale through your nose and exhale through your mouth.
- If you notice any tension in your body, breathe a sense of relaxation into that part of your body, and as you exhale, release the tension.
- When you become aware of thoughts, simply return your attention to your breath.

Day 4: Place signs around your home and workplace that say "Now." Each time you see one of the signs, bring your attention to now.

Day 5: Use your present to inform each conversation and activity you are involved with during the day. When you get in your car to drive to the supermarket, stop for a moment, take a deep breath, and for thirty seconds see yourself arriving safely at your destination. Just before you begin a performance appraisal meeting with one of your employees, stop for a moment, take a deep breath, and use the power of now for a thirty-second visualization of a successful outcome to the meeting. You may see you and your employee smiling at each other at the end of the meeting, hearing yourself say, "I am glad we had this opportunity to discuss your performance," and feeling satisfied.

Day 6: Live each moment as if it were your last. I have heard that the Angel of Death is always over our left shoulder. How would you seize the moment if this were true?

Three months before my mother's death, she was in an intensive care unit in the hospital. Her doctor told me that being ninety-two years old, she was quite weak, and that death was near. One of her nurses asked to talk with me. She asked me if I knew what was going on. We spoke for a while and she said that while my mom might not pass on today or tomorrow, from her experience, my mom was letting go. The moment became alive. During the next five days, my mom stayed in intensive care. In the presence of the Angel of Death, Love was alive. My mother was so happy to have her children with her. She spoke on the phone with all her friends and family. Being with her was the most loving experience I had ever known. What I learned is that the Angel of Death is nothing to fear, because in its presence, love is alive. This doesn't mean that you have to die tomorrow to feel love in the moment. It is a reminder that when you allow each moment to die, give way to the next, and live fully in the present with the knowledge that each moment is precious and may be your last, you have direct access to the power of now.

Day 7: Reflect and write your response to the following questions:

- What did you learn about yourself and the power of the present?
- How can you use these insights in your daily life—beginning now?

There are fine things which you mean to do some day, under what you think will be more favorable circumstances. But the only time that is surely yours is the present, hence this is the time to speak the word of appreciation and sympathy, to do the generous deed, to forgive the fault of a thoughtless friend, to sacrifice self a little more for others. Today is the day in which to express your noblest qualities of mind and heart, to do at least one worthy thing which you have long postponed, and to use your God-given abilities for the enrichment of someone less fortunate. Today you can make your life significant and worthwhile. The present is yours to do with as you will.

—GRENVILLE KLEISER

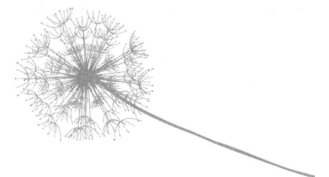

WEEK 36

Experience the Power of Movies

Movies are the most electrifying communications medium ever devised and the natural conduit for inspiring ourselves to look into the eternal issues of who we are and why we are here.

— STEPHEN SIMON

Going to the movies is a wonderful way to engage and connect with a story that can excite you, dazzle you, open your heart, and remind you of the magnificence as well as the destructiveness of human beings. Movies are the modern-day version of gathering around the campfire and hearing stories. They are fairy tales, and rather than being passed on through an oral tradition, they invade our senses with 3-D, surround sound, and visual effects that at times seem to reach out to us in our seats. (Keep in mind that fairy tales are stories that speak to the soul's journey and it is their deeper meaning that engages the soul in ways that are usually not immediately apparent.) On a big screen, stories are bigger than life and a slice of life, visual and auditory representations of thoughts that spring from the minds of people.

Movies can be a glorious escape from whatever circumstances you are in the midst of and can also touch you emotionally and wake you up from the daily drama of your own life. Movies can surprise you and embed images in your mind that capture your attention. Depending on what these images are, the road to fear or love is illuminated. Movies show us the full range of what is possible in terms of what the human mind can create and the experiences that human beings have in life. This week, use movies to open your eyes to what is possible. As you watch the movies and enjoy and reflect on their stories, remember that your life is an unfolding story and that you are the screenwriter, the producer, the director, and the leading character in the movie of your life. With this in mind, what movies would you like to watch to give yourself ideas for the movie of your life?

How to Do It

Day 1: Make a list of your all-time favorite movies, and next to each one, jot down what makes it special to you. Does it make you laugh out loud? Are you inspired by it? Norman Cousins writes in his book *Anatomy of an Illness* of the power of laughter in treating and curing a life-threatening tissue disease he had. He watched Marx Brothers movies from his hospital bed. In the midst of serious illness, movies provided the focus for him to laugh, laugh, and laugh. Here are some of my favorites, with a brief description of why I like them:

- *The Matrix*—creating our experience
- *Where Dreams Come From*—the power of thought in creating our experience
- *Life as a House*—how people's lives are changed in the presence of love
- *Pay It Forward*—the power of each of us to change the world
- *Beauty and the Beast*—the power of love
- *Monsters, Inc.*—how our thoughts feed our fears
- *Forrest Gump*—being who you are and always doing your best
- *Dead Man Walking*—seeing everyone as an expression of God
- *Road to Perdition*—fathers and sons; the life-giving power of love and the destructive power of jealousy and envy
- *Monsoon Wedding*—the healing power of love
- *Resurrection*—fear of love and the healing power of love
- *Starman*—fear of the unknown
- *Keeping the Faith*—the power of faith
- *Rabbit-Proof Fence*—the desire to be free
- *I AM*—what is right with the world

Day 2: Choose a movie from your list and watch it. Make yourself comfortable. Pop some popcorn and allow the movie to capture your attention.

Day 3: Go to the movies—or Netflix, Amazon, or Hulu—and see a movie that you might not ordinarily see. If you usually don't see movies with subtitles, treat yourself to one today; see an animated movie or an action movie. Experiment and allow the movie to tell you its story without judging it because it isn't the kind of movie you usually see.

Day 4: Ask five people today what their three all-time favorite movies are and why. Then watch one of them.

Day 5: If you have home movies, watch some. Allow this trip down memory lane to remind you of different times in your life. Many years after my husband, Byll, and I divorced, he sent me a video compilation of movies from the years we were married. It is something I treasure, a reminder of glorious times and adventures we had. Long after the *ouch* of the divorce had healed, what remained was reminders of good times. If by chance you are holding on to old pains, it is possible that seeing some videos of times you enjoyed can serve as a reminder that your past was also filled with happy times. If you don't have home movies to watch, journey through some photo albums of your life.

It is important to remember that you have the ability to experience greater personal freedom in your life when you free yourself from the resentments and wounds of your past—the movie reel (real?) that runs in your mind about your personal story. You have an opportunity to change your experience of your past by what you choose to remember and the story you tell yourself about it. So choose to remember the scenes of life that are empowering, and forgive and put to rest the others.

Day 6: Write a script for the movie of you, living a whole-hearted life. Describe your life through this script. Who are the other characters? What is the storyline? Write a scene that has you in the leading role of the life you choose to create.

Day 7: Reflect and write your response to the following question:

- How can you use this idea of going to the movies to enhance your peace and happiness?

Make a list of "Movies I Wanna See" and see them.

Is This Real?

My oldest sister, Ruth, often took me to the movies when I was a child. There were double features then and we would be in the theater for many hours. I remember often turning to her, tapping her on the arm, and whispering, "Is this really happening right now? Is this really going on in real life?" It took me quite a while to learn that the movie reel and real life were two different things. This continues to be helpful for me today when I remember that the stories of my life, my interpretations of events, are like a movie reel and that I can change those reels.

WEEK 37

Do Your Best

Your best is going to change from moment to moment;
it will be different when you are healthy as opposed to
sick. Under any circumstance, simply do your best, and
you will avoid self-judgment, self-abuse, and regret.

—DON MIGUEL RUIZ

Doing your best is about taking action, accepting, and enjoying the journey along the way. Doing your best is a cornerstone of living a wholehearted life. Doing your best is not about always being the first in your class, winning the prize, or getting the reward, although that is what your best might be. Doing your best is about doing *your* best. Your best may change from day to day. On a day when you wake up feeling great, your best will be different from your best on a day when you wake up with the flu. When you are experiencing a personal crisis, your best will be something else.

When you make a personal commitment to always

do your best, you use the present moment in determining your best rather than relying on an outside standard of what someone else is doing or the way you think it should be done. When you accept that you are doing your best, there is no reason to beat yourself up and judge yourself because you should have done it differently. You did your best.

All too often we judge our performance by an outside standard of success and accomplishment rather than what our personal best is at any given moment. This is learned behavior. As a child you may have come home with four A's on your report card and one B+. All you can remember of that experience is your father asking, "Why did you only get a B+ in biology?" Since that time, all you have been able to see is what you don't accomplish, what isn't good enough.

If you are plagued with a perfectionist gene, it is possible that nothing is ever good enough for you. You may constantly see your own actions as falling short of the way they should have been done, and you may not trust anyone else to get the job done. You are so focused on what is not working that you fail to see accomplishments and success right in front of you.

Many years ago, when my youngest stepson was six years old, I saw how my perfectionism was getting in the way of both allowing help and enjoying myself. I was making dinner, and it was Gabe's turn to set the table. I had placed the silverware in the center of the table for him. While he was setting the table, I was preparing the food, and my back was to him. Within a few moments, he told me he was finished and was going back to the den. I said, "Okay," and continued making dinner. A few minutes later, I went to the table and noticed that he had placed the forks on the wrong side of the plates. I was annoyed and started mumbling to myself, "If I want anything done right, I have to do it myself. Doesn't anybody in this house know how to do anything the right way?"

As I kept repeating these thoughts, remembering loads of evidence from the past to prove that I was right, I heard myself and realized how absolutely ridiculous I was being. He had done his best. The table was set. The placement of the forks on my dinner table was not going to cause demerits on my permanent record. If it was so important that the fork be on the left side of the plate, I could show him next time. I began to giggle at myself, amused at how I could so easily turn the simplest situation into a major production. This was a powerful lesson for me. I saw that often the task is done and it is done just fine, but my limited idea of what is acceptable blocks my ability to see that the best is already accomplished.

When you do your best, you are forgiving and accepting, and you do the best that is possible each and every day, whatever that may be. If you could have done it differently at the time you did it, then you would have! So commit to doing your best and notice how self-abuse, judgments of self and others, guilt, and shame melt away and you experience greater peace of mind and joy.

How to Do It

Day 1: Anytime you notice yourself judging yourself or others for what should have been done differently, say to yourself, "I did my best" or "She did her best."

Day 2: Assess your life in terms of the following areas and reflect on whether or not you are doing your best. Are you so focused on some areas that you are neglecting others? What would be a happier balance for you? Make a list of changes you want to make, and make them. Remember, this is not a task for judging yourself. Rather, it is an opportunity to see if you are doing your best to live the life you desire.

- Self-care
- Family
- Health
- Work
- Finances
- Fun and recreation
- Friendships
- Personal development
- Spirituality

Day 3: Answer these questions:

- What blocks you from doing your best?
- How can you use these blocks as stepping stones to doing your best?
- What gifts are these blocks offering you the opportunity to notice?
- What support do you need to do your best?

- How can you get or whom can you ask for this support?

Day 4: Do your best at honoring your body today. Brush and floss your teeth. Express your gratitude for your body in your actions: Wear comfortable shoes; eat delicious, nourishing food; use a great moisturizer on your skin; get a massage; take a refreshing shower; take a luxurious bath, smile at yourself when you look in a mirror.

Day 5: Do your best at asking for what you need. This is an area that many people find challenging. They think doing their best means doing it themselves. This is a self-defeating idea. Ask for help when you need it and accept it graciously.

Day 6: Create a "Doing My Best" credo. What defines your best? Write it, date it, sign it, and live it. Read it daily and make a copy of it for your wallet so you see it every time you reach for money, as a reminder that this, too, is something of value. Read it to your family and friends and ask them to gently remind you of it, if you forget. And when you do forget, simply get back on the horse.

Day 7: Reflect on and write your response to the following questions:

- What did you learn?
- How do you feel when you do your best?
- What do you want to remember and practice about doing your best that would be helpful in your daily life?

233

Creed for Optimists

by Christian D. Larson

Promise Yourself:

To be so strong that nothing can disturb your peace of mind.

To talk health, happiness, and prosperity to every person you meet.

To make all your friends feel that there is something worthwhile in them.

To look at the sunny side of everything and make your optimism come true.

To think only of the best, to work only for the best, and to expect only the best.

To be just as enthusiastic about the success of others as you are about your own.

To forget the mistakes of the past and press on to the greater achievements of the future.

To wear a cheerful expression at all times and give a smile to every living creature you meet.

To give so much time to improving yourself that you have no time to criticize others.

To be too large for worry, too noble for anger, too strong for fear, and too happy to permit the presence of trouble.

To think well of yourself and to proclaim this fact to the world, not in loud word, but in great deeds.

To live in the faith that the whole world is on your side, so long as you are true to the best that is in you.

WEEK 38
Give Compliments

> Compliment: an expression of esteem, respect, affection or admiration; an admiring remark, formal and respectful recognition.
>
> —MERRIAM-WEBSTER'S
> COLLEGIATE DICTIONARY

Giving compliments is a gift of recognition and acknowledgement. Both the giver and the receiver benefit from the energetic exchange of this gift. When people are asked what contributes to their experience of happiness, the gift of recognition and appreciation, precious expressions of love, is high on their list.

The challenge is that although recognition and appreciation are greatly desired, often the receiver of the compliment is uncomfortable and embarrassed about receiving the compliment. This happens in ordinary circumstances—for instance, you have recently had a haircut and someone at work says to you, "Your hair looks great." Instead of simply saying "Thank you," you go into a whole story about how it will really look better in a few weeks after it grows out a bit. Or a neighbor expresses his appreciation for your helpfulness and your reply is, "Oh, it was nothing." That response is a direct undermining of the power of the compliment and the appreciation that was given to you. In focusing on giving compliments, you direct your attention towards appreciation.

This week, give compliments, and if someone says to you, "Oh, it was nothing," reply by saying, "It was something to me, and I appreciate you." And while you are focused on giving compliments, open yourself to receiving the ones that are sent in your direction.

How to Do It

Day 1: Check out the Automatic Flatterer website, and visit it three times today. Notice how you feel, and forward it to others. http://www.cse.unsw.edu.au/~geoffo/humour/flattery.html

Day 2: When you wake up and before you go to sleep, compliment yourself. In the morning as you are looking in the mirror, spend five minutes complimenting your body for its magnificence: "I appreciate you, lungs, for working so elegantly and effortlessly; I appreciate you, my beautiful feet, for each and every day moving me from one place to the next; thank you, ears, for the great job you do hearing; thanks, stomach, for letting me know when I am full," and so forth. At night before you go to sleep, compliment yourself: "Thank you, sense of humor, for reminding me to lighten up; thank you, eyes, hands, and feet for your great teamwork today."

Day 3: Make an appreciation journal for someone you care about. Use www.CelebrateAHero.com or make your own. This is an opportunity to express your love and appreciation. This can also be a wonderful gift for birthdays, weddings, anniversaries, Mother's Day, Father's Day, or any day you want to express your love and appreciation for someone in your life.

Day 4: Give compliments. Wherever you are today, give at least one compliment: in the supermarket, at the post office, at work, at home, at the bank—and remember to include the customer service representative you spoke with on the phone—and so forth.

Day 5: Write and mail three compliment letters: to a family member, a friend, and someone you don't know personally who is an important influence in your life, perhaps a particular author, a celebrity whose work has inspired you, or someone in your town whom you admire.

Day 6: Compliment people who impact your daily life so invisibly that you may not think about them regularly: the postal worker who delivers your mail, the person who picks up your trash, the bus drivers who deliver you to and from work, your boss, the person who stocks the shelves in the supermarket. Make a list of all the people who make your life easier, whom you don't often see, and compliment them. If you don't see them all today, focus on complimenting them during this month.

Day 7: Reflect and write your response to the following questions:

- What did you become aware of?
- How do you feel about giving compliments? Receiving compliments?
- What will you continue to do?

> After my father had seen me in five or six things, he said, "Son, your mother and I really enjoyed your recent film, and I must say that you're a lot like John Wayne." And I said, "How so?" And he said, "Well, you're exactly the same in all your roles." Now, as a modern American actor, that's not what you want to hear. But for a guy who watched John Wayne movies and grew up in Iowa, it's a sterling compliment.
>
> —DERMOT MULRONEY

WEEK 39

Ignite the Full Resources of Your Imagination

Imagination is the voice of daring. If there is anything Godlike about God, it is that he dared to imagine everything.

—HENRY MILLER

Imagine your wholehearted life. Dream your heartfelt desires. Pretend you are a mighty expression of love. Your imagination is your most powerful natural resource. It is the starting point of all that you experience. Unfortunately, out of habit, we use our imagination to reactivate our history and repeat old patterns of fear and lack rather than to dream our future anew. When you use your imagination in service of your heartfelt desires, when you dream dreams that spring forth from your Heartsong, when you act as if you are love, then peace and happiness are yours for the choosing. Remember, your life is your greatest and most miraculous artistic creation.

Creation begins with a spark of desire. That spark

may be ignited because something in your life is not satisfying. You experience lack, unhappiness, and dissatisfaction, and in an instant, a heartfelt idea surfaces. Or in the quiet of meditation, in the full silence of a walk on the beach, bathed in the light of the full moon, or embraced and consumed in the loving energy of intimacy, an idea captures your attention. With the spark of desire alive, your imagination is the resource that gives it legs and begins to root your Heartsong, first as the blueprint of an idea within, then in physical reality.

Using the full resources of your imagination, you create an image, a scene of your desire as fully accomplished: You see what it looks like; you hear the sounds of your dream fully accomplished; you taste the flavors, smell the fragrances, and with a clear sense of your dream, you step into the scene created by your imagination and experience your desire as occurring at this very moment.

Through the conscious use of your imagination, you activate powerful thought forms that are energetically charged with our faith and conviction. These thought forms are like rockets that are released into the Greater Field of Life—the universe that constantly sings one song, one verse, a uni-verse: *Yes.*

When you engage in this conscious imagining for a minimum of one minute each day, you create your life anew, again, and again, and again. So imagine; be childlike in your playful ability to pretend. This is the prep work for what you *intend* (*tending* to from the *inside*) to birth in your daily experience. Act as if your dreams are alive right now (since they are), and live your life with the authority of your active imagination. You are the author of your life, and your imagination is in the service of your wholehearted life vision.

How to Do It

Day 1: Consciously use your imagination three times today to create your experience. Since we are constantly creating our experience through our thoughts, charged with our emotional energy, the crucial component of this exercise is to be conscious of what you imagine. For example, when you wake up in the morning and think about the healthy eating plan you began, you notice that you are feeling a bit anxious about following it. Use your imagination. For one minute, focus on a scene of your desire fulfilled—and focus on your desire in the past tense, as though it is already accomplished (Letting your mind practice experiencing something new already done is powerful mind training). Use the following format to prepare your visualization:

Desire: I easily followed my healthy eating plan today and I feel terrific.

Scene of Desire Accomplished: It is nighttime and I am in my bathroom, wearing my favorite comfortable yellow cotton tee shirt and soft, blue-and-yellow-striped flannel pajama bottoms. I see my smiling face in the mirror. I hear the sound of running water. My mouth has the fresh clean taste of toothpaste. I am saying to myself, "Good for me! I easily followed my healthy delicious eating plan today. I feel great."

Use this model to identify your intention and create a scene that reflects the fulfillment of your desire for any situation that you are going into: finding a parking space, writing a report at work, having a conversation with your child, making vacation plans with your spouse. Use your imagination to *live into* your life. This is particularly powerful when you notice that you are experiencing doubt, fear, or anxiety about something. Stop, identify your desire, and write or imagine a description, using as much detail as possible, of your desire fully accomplished. (Make sure to include yourself in the scene!) For one minute, using the full resources of your imagination, live the scene of your desire accomplished.

Imagine a sign: *Daydreaming Allowed Here.*

Day 2: Make a collage of your heart's desire fully accomplished. Do not limit yourself to what you think is possible—allow your imagination to supply the images of your Heartsong. (Last night, at a dinner party, I heard about a man who is blind and skis in the Special Olympics!) This is a collage of what your dream is, not how you are going to get there. Ask yourself the question: "What is my heart's desire?" as you choose pictures from magazines, newspapers, greeting cards, and photos for your collage. Trust your instinct as you cut and paste. Allow your collage to illuminate and articulate your heart's desire for you. Hang the collage someplace where you can see it and silently spend five minutes each day stepping into your dream.

Day 3: Create your heart's desire. Draw a heart and write a specific desire in the center. Draw lines from the center of your heart extending outside of the heart all around it. On each line, write a clear description of your desire accomplished. Beginning today, spend at least five minutes in the morning and five minutes in the evening focusing on this expression of your wholehearted life accomplished. As you move around your heart in your imagination, know that your heart's desire is created.

I am My Perfect Body Weight

My thoughts are an expression of loving my Body

Everything I eat turns to Health & Beauty

I easily exercise 5 times a week

I feel comfortable and attractive in my clothes

I am healthy

I am strong, flexible and well-toned

I'm comfortable, graceful and at ease in my body

When I see myself in the mirror I say "I'm beautiful"

I eat delicious and nutritious meals

I'm sexy

I Easily Express My Love

I let people know what I appreciate about them

I keep my word

I make time to be with people I love

I say "I love you" before I end a phone call with my family and friends

I give compliments

I listen when a friend is upset

I hold the door open for someone carrying heavy packages

I say thank you and smile to express my appreciation

I take a bubble bath at the end of a busy day

I hug my kids daily

Day 4: Write a letter to yourself, dated one year from today. Describe your life, in the present tense, and include your accomplished dreams in this description. Read the letter aloud (*allowed*) until you experience the joy and pleasure, the peace and happiness of living your Heartsong. Burn the letter, knowing that you have participated in a powerful ritual of your intention to live your dreams. Sprinkle the ashes in the soil of a plant, and know that your dreams are seeded and fertilized.

Day 5: Find quotations and phrases that remind you of the power of imagining, daydreaming, and pretending. Display these quotations as reminders to use the full resources of your imagination to inform and create your daily experience. Here are some I've found:

- *Live out of your imagination, not your history.* —STEPHEN R. COVEY
- *The man who has no imagination has no wings.* —MUHAMMAD ALI
- *A rock pile ceases to be a rock pile the moment a single man contemplates it, bearing within him the image of a cathedral.* —ANTOINE DE SAINT-EXUPÉRY
- *I saw the angel in the marble and carved until I set him free.* —MICHAELANGELO
- *All men who have achieved great things have been great dreamers.* —ORISON SWETT MARDEN

Day 6: Listen to John Lennon's song "Imagine," read Martin Luther King, Jr.'s "I Have a Dream" speech, and imagine the world you desire. Rather than filling your mind with violent images on TV/online news and in the newspapers today, imagine the world news that you would produce. See it, hear it, taste it, smell it, feel it, be it.

Day 7: Write a poem, a song, or an essay on imagining and share it with three people. Reflect and write your response to the following questions:

- What did you learn?
- How can you use the full resources of your imagination to live your wholehearted life?

> Visualize your wishes in your mind's eye.... Visualize what it is you want with all your heart. See it with your inner sight and feel it as if you were really there, experiencing it with all your senses. Practice visualization every day. Our dreams help us to create our material reality as surely as our material reality helps us to create our dreams.
>
> —MONTE FARBER
> AND AMY ZERNER

WEEK 40
Pray

And all things, whatsoever ye shall ask in prayer, believing, ye shall receive.

—MATTHEW 21:12

I believe prayer is the sending out of vibrations from one person to another and to God. All the universe is in vibration.

—NORMAN VINCENT PEALE

Prayer is a powerful form of communion with God, Source Energy, the Loving Energy of the universe. When wedded with faith, prayer is a gateway to living a wholehearted life of authenticity, passion, and purpose. Every religious tradition has its own form of prayer, all of which create a bridge between you and the divine, so that there is communion (common union) between the two. When you say a prayer of petition, asking for something for yourself or others, you are asking God, the Source Energy of the universe of which we are a part, to focus its energy on your desire.

When you have faith (believing in something 100

percent) that your prayers are heard and are being answered, your only work is to allow your mind to be in a vibration of receiving and allowing (to experience the result you desire). The energetic universe, your co-creative partner, will provide direction and steps for you to take for your prayers to be answered.

Examples of this occur regularly in daily life. You are late for an appointment and unable to find a parking space, so you say a little prayer to easily get a parking space and get to your appointment on time. You feel a nudge to turn down a street you have already been down three times, and there it is, your parking space. When you arrive for your appointment ten minutes late, you find out that the person you are meeting had to take an emergency phone call and will be with you within the next five minutes. It all worked out. Prayer focused your attention on your desire, and your faith opened the space for your desire to be manifest.

From 1982 to 1983, a ten-month survey was conducted at San Francisco General Hospital on a group of 393 cardiac patients. Strangers prayed for one half of the group, who didn't know they were being prayed for. The other half of the group did not receive prayers. The results showed that those who did receive prayers needed fewer antibiotics and less assistance with breathing. This study, described in the book *Healing Prayers* by Dr. Larry Dossey, supports the relationship between prayer and well-being. Today, an ever-increasing number of medical schools offer courses in religion, spirituality, and the mind-body connection. This week, do your own experiment. Focus on prayer, and notice the power of this tool in your life.

> Prayer does not change God, but it changes him who prays.
>
> —SØREN KIERKEGAARD

How to Do It

Day 1: Start and end your day with a prayer of appreciation. You may do this in front of your altar, down on your knees at the side of your bed, or standing at the window looking outside at the glorious day. Do this when you wake up, before you do anything else, and just before you go to sleep.

In Judaism, the traditional morning practice includes the following parts (adapted from *The Busy Soul* by Rabbi Terry Bookman):

- Prayer of gratitude: "I am grateful to You, dear God, Giver and Sustainer of life, for having granted me another day of life. Your Love and Faith in me encourage and inspire me."
- Daily self check-in:
  - Think about your body's health and the way it functions well, even when some parts of it do not. Offer appreciation to Source Energy for your physical health and well-being.
  - Think about your mind and its ability to learn and be open to new ideas. Offer thanks to God for your mind and your ability to think and grow in wisdom and understanding.
  - Think about what actions you take in

loving service to others. What do you do to bring love and healing to our world? Offer gratitude to the Source of Life for your capacity to love and be loved, and to be a blessing to yourself and others through kindness and service.

o Experience your connection with all that is. Know that each thought you think, each word you say, and each action you do affects the whole of life on earth. Offer thanks to God for your awareness and oneness with all that is.

- Meditation: Read inspiring words and reflect on how they apply to you today.

Your nighttime prayer may be a simple expression of gratitude for all that you have been offered and received during the day. The prayer I often say as I am drifting off to sleep is this: "Thank you, God, for another day of loving."

Day 2: Use prayer spontaneously throughout the day when you notice you are off-center and feeling victim to the circumstances and conditions of your life. As soon as you notice you are aggravated, annoyed, frustrated, critical, or judgmental, say a prayer. Your prayer may be as simple as, "Loving energy of the universe guide me through this challenge," or it may be the repetition of a familiar prayer such as the Serenity Prayer by Reinhold Niebuhr:

God grant me the serenity
to accept the things I cannot change,
The courage to change the things I can,
And the wisdom to know the difference.

Or make up your own spontaneous prayer in the moment for the circumstances you are presented with. A few years ago, when I was driving in my car, without a GPS and lost, I yelled aloud to God, bellowing "God dammit!" as though I was blaming God in the midst of my dilemma. After a few minutes, I realized God was exactly who I needed to call upon since my self-talk was critical of my being lost and not knowing the way. It occurred to me that I yelled out to God in a loud voice so I could be reminded to engage with Source Energy above the chatter that was filling my mind. I took a deep breath, laughing at myself, and said, "God, guide me." Within moments I saw a sign for the road I was looking for!

Day 3: Take a prayer you are familiar with, one you may have learned as a child by rote, and say it, read it, allow the words to come alive in you. In the Christian tradition, this is an example of the practice of Lectio Divina, which means "divine reading." This practice is a means of developing a deeply personal and intimate relationship with God. In the words of Marina Wiederkehr from *The Song of the Seed*:

Lectio is a way of reading with the heart. It is a contemplative way
of reflecting on the Scriptures or other spiritual classics...
When you romance the Word, you...ponder it, pray it,

sing it,
study it, love it....Listen to it with the ear of your heart.
Cling to it as a beloved. Cherish it. Become a home for it.

Day 4: Say a prayer before each meal. This is an act of gratitude, an opportunity to connect with all that has contributed in bringing the food to you, and a chance to recognize the food as the nourishment it is. I used to feel put on the spot when someone asked me to say grace. Then one day, as I sat at the table by myself, I decided to say a prayer before I ate. I sat in silence, and this is the prayer that presented itself to me:

I thank all the elements for bringing this to food to me.
The Earth for the soil that nourishes the plants and gives them a place to grow.
The Water that nourishes the plants and animals with water.
The Sun that shines its light on all that grows.
The Air that spreads the seeds and through its breath gives this food strength.
I thank all the people involved in bringing this food to me today, including the check-out people at the supermarket. The ancestors and offspring of the people who planted the seeds. The driver who delivered the food to my local market.
May this food nourish and expand my experience of Love in all that I think, say, see, hear, touch, smell, taste, feel and do.
And so it is.

Day 5: Say the *Prayer for Wholehearted Living* (page xxx) once an hour today.

Day 6: Create a prayer ritual that you can incorporate into your life as a daily spiritual practice. Examples of this may include the following:

- A specific prayer you say each morning and evening
- A daily practice of appreciation for the gifts in your life
- The use of a specific prayer (Prayer for Wholehearted Living, Serenity Prayer, The Lord's Prayer, and so forth) whenever you notice you are out of connection with Source Energy
- Spending time in nature to feel your connection with the natural world
- A specific prayer time each day when you pray for the highest good for those you love, and for peace and happiness for all beings

Day 7: Reflect and write your response to the following questions:

- What did you notice this week about the power of prayer in your life?
- How did you use prayer as a tool this week to strengthen your connection with the God of your understanding, the Loving Energy of the Universe?
- How do you plan to incorporate prayer in your life?

God scattered holy sparks all over the world. Whenever a person prays with intent, his words attract one of these sparks and propel it heavenward to add brilliance and sparkle to God's glorious crown.

—ARVEI NACHAL,
COMMENTARY ON THE TALMUD

WEEK 41
Detach and Let Go

In our willingness to step into the unknown, the field of
all possibilities, we surrender ourselves to the creative
mind that orchestrates the dance of the universe.

— DEEPAK CHOPRA

Detaching and letting go is how we release from the
past, unhook from unsatisfying habits of thought and
behavior, and live life fully in the precious present. Many
of us begin each new day loaded down with emotional
baggage, limiting beliefs, and expectations based on
past circumstances that we define as truth. These attach-
ments to circumstances, relationships, addictions, and
patterns of thought and behavior are often experienced
as a lifetime prison sentence with occasional moments
off for good behavior. As human beings, we follow the
path of least resistance in our thoughts and actions,
which means we repeat patterns and habits on auto-

matic, without thinking, in a sleep state even though our eyes are wide open. To create a new pattern requires the conscious focus of your attention on what you feel and what you think, say, and do. To focus your attention requires a commitment to being awake and aware in the present; it requires you to access your personal power. The paradox is that your energy is already being used to hold the old patterns and habits in place. It is as though you are caught in a spider's web, and to detach and let go you have to free yourself from each thin sticky thread of the web. Sometimes, you can go right to the central thread, which is some variation of "I am not enough" or "I'm not okay." By detaching from these ideas, you automatically let go of patterns and behaviors that were dependent on that core idea for their nourishment and survival. This week, as you detach and let go, you are saying *yes* to a deeper and fuller experience of personal freedom—and isn't this what wholehearted living is all about?

This is not the time to judge and beat yourself up for limiting beliefs and lousy habits. Don't use this week's exercises to prove to yourself that since you are still stuck, you will always be stuck. Instead, enjoy this opportunity to free up your energy, make conscious choices, and detach and let go.

How to Do It

Day 1: Today is the day to detach and let go of stuff. You may choose your email inbox, your closet, your medicine cabinet, or your underwear drawer. Choose something that makes you feel overwhelmed by the clutter and burdened by the disorganization. Clean it out. Let go of stuff. Notice the infusion of energy you feel when you are finished. Close the drawer, leave the room, and the next time you open the drawer or enter the room, feel a greater lightness and sense of accomplishment filling your being. If you notice that, rather than feeling the freedom of letting go, you are being abusive to yourself for waiting so long to do this, stop it. You did it today; this counts. The past is over, so let it go.

Day 2: Choose one person or situation in your life to let go of. For instance, if you're still angry at your former spouse, from whom you've been divorced for four years, let go of this anger. If you have wanted to lose weight for years and every diet you go on lasts no longer than a week or two, let go of the self-hate cycle that operates on automatic. If your financial situation keeps you up at night with worry and anxiety, find ways to move through this problem, starting with your relationship with money. If all of this applies to you, for the sake of this exercise, choose only one to begin with, or you'll be in such a quandary about which one to choose that you'll exhaust yourself without doing the exercise!

Once you've chosen a situation:

- Sit comfortably.
- Close your eyes.
- Focus on your breath.
- Take three full, deep breaths. Breathe in through your nose a sense of calming relaxation, and exhale fully and deeply through your mouth, allowing yourself to relax fully into the support of the chair beneath your body and the floor beneath your feet.
- Using the full resources of your imagination, see

yourself attached by a thread, rope, cable, or web to the situation or person that is worrying you and draining your energy. Simply notice the connection between you and the situation.

- Take a pair of scissors or metal cable cutters and cut the thread from where it connects to your body.

- When you have cut the thread of connection, see the situation or person, like a helium balloon that has been released, begin to disappear from your sight as it drifts up and away, getting smaller and smaller and until it is gone.

- Focus your attention on the places where the thread was connected to your body. If there are remnants of the thread within you still, gently take them out and drop them to the earth.

- Feel lightness in your being and an infusion of energy.

- Gently open your eyes, feeling better than before.

- Use this technique anytime you are attached to something, as a way of detaching and letting go. By freeing up your energy from your connection to your worry and fear, you now have greater access to energy to focus your attention on what you *do* want to create in the present moment.

Day 3: Use the "Oops" technique. Anytime you notice you are caught in a web of abusive and judgmental thoughts about yourself or others, simply say "Oops" (aloud or to yourself), and get on a new train of thought. Approach this as though you have simply made a wrong turn; all you have to do is say "Oops" as you get back on track with thoughts that enhance your experience right now.

Day 4: Practice detaching and letting go of habits today by doing things differently. This is actually practice in increasing your flexibility, something that aids in detaching and letting go. If you usually brush your teeth with your right hand, use your left. Hold your phone to the other ear. If you wear a watch or bracelet, switch it to your other wrist. Use your non-dominant hand to hold a spoon. Use the elliptical trainer at the gym rather than the treadmill. Put a sock on your left foot first. Be creative. You will probably notice that you feel odd and uncomfortable when you make these changes. This is ordinary, because when you detach and let go of habits you are used to doing on automatic—when you are in a trance—the new behavior does feel awkward, simply because you are not used to it. If you continue with some of these changes regularly, you will notice that in a short time, the new behaviors become your default. For some this will only take a few days. You may want to make some of these changes every week, to expand your flexibility.

Day 5: Use your feelings as your guidance system to let you know when you are attached to something. Whenever you are consumed by unhappiness, sadness, anger, loneliness, or any feelings that create a personal hell, this is a pretty good indicator that you are attached to an idea that is draining your energy. When you notice any of these feelings today, use the "Oops" technique and focus your attention on a new thought that feels more satisfying. This doesn't mean that you will never have an unhappy feeling again. It means that you can use your feelings as a guidance system and make choices about where you continue to focus your attention. Recently, I was missing my mom, who died in 2001, and I noticed that I was beginning to settle into feeling miserable. There was a domino effect, as I began to feel blue about many other situations and circumstances. I noticed that I was allowing my sadness free rein to take me on a roller coaster ride. I took a deep breath and began having a conversation in my mind with my mom. Within minutes, I had a smile on my face, remembering special times with her. I had felt my sadness and used it to move into a deeper experience of my mom's presence.

Day 6: On the left side of a page, make a list of thoughts and behaviors that you have been attached to that do not serve you. When you have completed that side of the page, go back to the first item, and beside it, write a new thought or behavior that is more supportive of your wholehearted life. Here are some examples:

I'm never gonna lose this weight.	*My body is beautiful, healthy, and fit.*
I'll be single forever.	*I'm in a loving relationship.*
My kids never listen to me.	*I love my communication with my kids.*
I get no recognition at work.	*I feel good about the job I do.*

This is practice in changing your programming, detaching and letting go of thoughts that reinforce what you don't want, and creating a new script, which will then direct your eyes to seeing your experience through a new point of view. Be playful. Remember that you are the dream and the dreamer of your life!

Day 7: Write a poem about detaching and letting go. Reflect and write your response to the following questions:

- What did you learn?
- How can you use the techniques you learned to detach and let go in your daily life?

> We must learn to let go, to give up, to make room for the things we have prayed for and desire.
>
> —CHARLES FILLMORE

7 Choices in the Process of Letting Go of Stuff

A "Letting Go" Tip
From Darren Johnson

1. *Acknowledge and Accept what you need to let go*
2. *Realize change is necessary*
3. *Change your internal conversation*
4. *Choose to Maintain a healthy attitude through the process*
5. *Choose to Focus on what you can control*
6. *Consciously choose to Let Go of what you cannot control*
7. *Create a Plan of action to move forward*

Modern-Day Transformations

When I finished writing this chapter, I took a writing rest, got some lunch, and began to watch the *Biggest Loser* episode that was on last night (season fifteen, episode thirteen). Here's something you may not have known about me: I'm a child of the fifties and I do love TV! It was makeover week. The seven remaining contestants were getting a makeover after becoming athletes and taking off between sixty and one hundred pounds during the past twelve weeks.

After negotiating with myself about how long I could watch before getting back to the next chapter, I watched through the contestants' meeting with their families after the big reveal. This is a modern-day transformation. While there is no question that there was a mighty change in each person's physical appearance, their inner transformations radiated through my iPad screen. If you have the opportunity, watch this episode. Watch it through the eyes of detaching and letting go. Watch it through eyes that see what is truly present when you say *yes* to life.

WEEK 42

Eat Dessert First

Save the good stuff for last?
Whose idea was that?

Eating dessert first is about having the good stuff first. Don't save it for a rainy day. Don't wait until tomorrow. Don't wait until you are the right weight, until your nails are the perfect length, until every issue in your life is worked out, or until you have the right amount of money in the bank. Do it now. Many people spend their lives waiting: waiting to get married, waiting to finish school, waiting to have kids, waiting until their children are grown, waiting until they retire...waiting, waiting, waiting. All we have is now. The past is over and the future lives in our imagination. Now is the precious present, a gift that contains all the power that ever was and ever will be. It is up to you to savor and delight in the present moment, to approach your life as a glorious, magnificent buffet, and to reach for and enjoy the feast before you. This week, eat dessert first, and as you eat it, enjoy it—this is the recipe for wholehearted living.

How to Do It

Day 1: Today, literally eat dessert first. Begin your meal with dessert. If you are truly bold, have a meal of dessert only. Think about what is dessert for you. Don't limit it to cake, sweets, or ice cream. What is something you would love to eat—something that makes you salivate simply by imagining it? As you eat dessert first, enjoy it. If you notice you are making deals with yourself about the diet you'll begin tomorrow, stop it. Enjoy, now. This is not about stuffing yourself and bingeing. This is about savoring, delighting, enjoying, and allowing.

Day 2: Think of something you have always wanted to do, but didn't think you had the time, the money, or the know-how for. Begin it today. If it's a trip you want to take, get information about it and mark it on your calendar. If it's a business you want to begin, see it as accomplished and take a step toward doing it. If it's a relationship you desire, start by enjoying your life today and use your imagination to *see* what you want. When you see loving relationships, enjoy the pleasure of seeing what is possible and know that it is on the menu of your life as well. Today, choose the dessert you truly desire.

Day 3: As you approach each activity of your day, consciously focus your attention on the "dessert" of the activity. As you get up and get ready for work, focus on how delicious it is to be beginning a new day. As you enter the farmers' market, delight in the opportunity to choose a variety of items to make a tasty meal. As you walk to your weekly department meeting, smile as you think about this opportunity to share your ideas. As you step into each segment of your day, intend to have dessert.

Day 4: Invite friends and/or family for dinner and serve dessert first. Share your thoughts about having dessert first and let each person present know the ways in which they are "dessert" in your life.

Day 5: Prepare a great dessert. This may be an old favorite that brings loving memories to mind, it may be something you always wanted to make, or it may be an old family recipe that fills your house with mouthwatering aromas. Yum.

Day 6: Give a dessert to someone whom you'd like to appreciate with a treat. Leave a special cookie for your mail carrier, give the receptionist in your office his favorite sweet, put a special dessert in your child's lunch box. Place a treat on your lover's pillow. Remember, what makes this dessert special is the love you put into it. So as you get it, prepare it, and deliver it, do it all with love.

Day 7: Reflect and write your response to the following questions:

- How can you keep this idea alive in your daily life?
- What did you learn?

When you finish writing, eat dessert first!

Feeding Body and Spirit

Soup is a dessert for me on cold winter days. It's not just eating it; it's also the preparation that makes my mouth water. When my stepkids were younger, I would dream up new soup recipes and feel a smile all over when they asked for seconds. As they got older, they would chop vegetables with me, and I cherished this time we had together in the kitchen. When my stepdaughter, Maya, moved to San Francisco, before she had children, I would often call her on a cold winter day as I was chopping vegetables for soup, and we would have the same kind of intimate heartwarming conversation we used to have when she was actually in the kitchen with me. And these days, whenever I visit my grandkids in San Francisco, we make a huge pot of soup together. It's become a ritual that feeds our bodies and our spirits.

WEEK 43

Be Silent

Do not the most moving moments of our lives find us all without words?

— MARCEL MARCEAU

We need to find God, and he cannot be found in noise and restlessness. God is the friend of silence. See how nature—trees, flowers, grass—grows in silence; see the stars, the moon and the sun, how they move in silence....We need silence to be able to touch souls.

— MOTHER TERESA

Being silent is a practice that opens you to a deep connection with both your inner and outer world. Most of our daily lives are filled with noise. Many of us begin our day with the buzz of an alarm clock, which is quickly replaced by the sound of a radio, music, or TV, which then serves as the background to electric razors, electric toothbrushes, running water, conversations in raised voices over the beep of a microwave, the hum of the refrigerator, the drip of the coffeemaker, the sloshing of the dishwasher—and all of this before we have even left the house.

All of this noise shuts down your sensitivity to the

natural sounds of the universe—the swoosh of the air through the trees, the conversations of birds, the sound of rain against your windows, or the purr of a cat. Most importantly, all the racket keeps the still small voice within still and small, outside the range of the cacophony to which you have become accustomed. Being silent opens a new world to you. If it is a world that has been masked for too long with noise, it will initially seem unfamiliar. This week, dare to explore this territory. Even if you have visited with it recently, approach it as a visitor and allow it to show you its treasures, which include the nurturing embrace of being wholehearted.

How to Do It

Day 1: Be silent for ten minutes twice today, and experiment with this as a daily practice. This isn't simply not talking. Place a "Do Not Disturb" sign on your door. Turn off the phone ringer. Close the windows against the street noise. Put your computer on sleep mode—better yet, turn it off. Sit in a comfortable chair. Close your eyes. Listen to the silence. You may notice that silence is very noisy. You may become aware of a judge inside of you commenting and criticizing this process by saying "This is taking forever; this is a waste of time; I could be doing something else right now; I'm uncomfortable sitting here," and so forth. As you become aware of this voice, detach and let go of the thoughts as you exhale. Focus your attention on the sound of your breath as it enters your body through your nose and leaves your body through your mouth. As sounds in the room hook your attention, notice them and refocus on your breath. At the end of ten minutes, slowly open your eyes, notice how you feel, and move gently and easily into whatever you are doing next. Give some thought to what you will use to let you know when ten minutes is up. You may want to set your smartphone to the sound of a harp or chime as your *time's up* indicator. You may experiment with giving yourself an instruction to easily and effortlessly open your eyes in ten minutes, and have faith in yourself to follow this instruction. This is a technique I use, and with practice, it is extremely reliable.

Day 2: Be silent during a meal. You may have to let your family members or roommates know that you are going to do this, and you may want to invite them to participate. Again, the judge who has been keeping up a steady monologue within you may capture your attention. Notice and breathe. You may become more aware of the taste of the food, the sound of the silverware touching your plate, the conversations around you. You may experience your whole being quiet down, or you may become impatient. Notice and be silent.

Day 3: Be silent from the time you wake up until you leave your house. Again, you may want to inform the people you live with that you are doing this. Don't turn on the TV, read the newspaper, or listen to music or the news. If others in your house are doing these things, focus your attention elsewhere. Focus instead on what you are actually involved with in the moment. Hear the sound of the shower, feel the water against your body. Can you hear the sound of your razor as you shave? Use your creativity in communicating with others.

Day 4: Only speak today when it is absolutely necessary. What do you notice? How much of your daily talk is really necessary?

Day 5: Sit in silence for thirty minutes.

Day 6: Be silent for the day. Let people you will be around know that you are having a day of silence from the time you wake up until the time you go to bed.

Day 7: Reflect and write your response to the following questions:

- How did being silent contribute to your peace of mind and well being?
- What did you learn?
- How can you apply these learnings to your daily life?

> A wise old owl sat on an oak;
> The more he saw the less he spoke;
> The less he spoke the more he heard;
> Why aren't we like that wise old bird?
> —ENGLISH NURSERY RHYME

> True silence is the rest of the mind; it is to the spirit what sleep is to the body, nourishment and refreshment.
>
> —WILLIAM PENN

WEEK 44

Take a Vacation

Every person needs to take one day away. A day in which one consciously separates the past from the future. Jobs, family, employers, and friends can exist one day without any one of us, and if our egos permit us to confess, they could exist eternally in our absence. Each person deserves a day away in which no problems are confronted, no solutions searched for. Each of us needs to withdraw from the cares which will not withdraw from us.

— MAYA ANGELOU

Taking a vacation—whether for an hour on a massage table, a long weekend at the beach, or a three-week holiday exploring foreign lands—is nourishment for living a wholehearted life. I took a vacation this morning. I hadn't realized as I drove to meet a friend that our morning walk in the woods would be a vacation, but it was. We parked our cars and set off on the trail, not sure where the path would lead us. It was one of those glorious summer mornings—sunny, clear, a breeze in the air. Ah, the joy of a new day, the beauty of nature.

As the trail became sandy, we thought we would soon be approaching the bay. And there it was. We weren't quite sure where we were, so we explored. And then she said, "You wanna go into the water?" My immediate reaction was to think "It's too chilly, we don't have towels," and then a surge of adventure filled me, and I said, "Yes." There we were in the water, wearing an assortment of underwear and workout clothes, and she called out, "I'm on vacation." A few miles from our homes, we were on vacation, experiencing pleasure and relaxation. So often the demands of daily life leave us depleted—yearning for the weekends to catch up on some rest, dreaming of the vacation we'll take next week, next month, or next year. By then we are so wound up that by the time we get into the rhythm of our vacation, it is time to go home again.

It seems to me that vacations start with our state of mind rather than a change of location, although a magnificent location can certainly provide the support for a vacation state of mind. It is possible to create mini-vacations in our lives that serve to refresh and renew. By the time I got home this morning from my unexpected vacation, I felt a sense of calm and relaxation that led me to get more done, more easily than on those days when I rush and feel harried. So this is your vacation week. It may not be a week at the beach or even a trip to a special vacation spot, but naming experiences as vacation will allow them to be pleasurable, renewing, and refreshing. I know that greater peace and happiness will be your travel companions as you take a vacation.

How to Do It

Day 1: Take a vacation in your mind. Imagine your most relaxing scene:

- Close your eyes.
- Take five deep breaths, inhaling a sense of relaxation through your nose and exhaling any undue stress or tension through your mouth, into the earth.
- Using the full resources of your imagination, create an image of your most relaxing scene.
- See your most relaxing scene, notice the colors, hear the sounds, smell the fragrances, taste the flavors, and feel the feelings. With a clear sense of this scene filling your being, step into your most relaxing scene. Experience your most relaxing scene. Do this for thirty to sixty seconds.
- Experience a sense of vitality and renewal.
- Take a deep breath and relax your focus.
- Focus your attention on your breath, inhaling and exhaling three times.
- At your own speed, gently open your eyes, feeling wide awake, better than before, alert and fully connected with yourself, and prepared for whatever is next in your day.

Use the technique in the morning, evening, and anytime during the day that you need a vacation. Practice it daily, and your most relaxing scene will be available as a natural resource, reminding you that you can always take a vacation in your mind. Remember, your being doesn't know the difference between being in far-off lands on a well-planned vacation or using your imagination to create a vacation.

Day 2: Turn your lunch hour into vacation time today. If it's a nice day, go to a nearby park or new café with outdoor seating and imagine you are on an avenue in Paris enjoying people-watching. If you love art and there is a nearby museum, go in and enjoy one great work of art that makes your heart sing. Use your imagination to turn your lunch hour into a glorious vacation. I used to meet my husband at his office in the midst of a busy day, and we'd go off for a forty-five-minute picnic. We'd find a grassy spot, put down a blanket, and enjoy what felt like a leisurely vacation lunch in the midst of our workday. (I like making a rule that there is no talk of work, kids, or home repairs during this vacation!)

Day 3: Plan a vacation. Search the internet, get information, ask family and friends about some of their favorite vacations, and plan a dream vacation. It may be as simple as a weekend in a nearby bed and breakfast to get a rest from your daily routine, or it may be a month-long trip that you have desired for years. Dream it, see it, and take action to live it.

Day 4: Take a pampering vacation today. Go for a manicure and pedicure and luxuriate in the experience. Get a massage. When you work out at the gym, give yourself some extra time to use the sauna or steam room. When the kids have gone to bed and you have finished everything you have to do for the day, take a hot bath using bubbles, your favorite oils, or a special soap. Light candles and turn off the lights, turn the phone ringer off, and feel the water embracing your body, washing tension down the drain.

Day 5: Approach your day as though you are on vacation, even if you are going to work, picking up the kids, seeing friends, and so forth. Do all your activities as though they are part of your vacation. If you ride public transportation, pretend this is the first time you have been on this bus route. Ask for directions as if you were on the Underground in London for the first time. If you drive, either take a new route, or actually look at where you are as you drive along this road you usually travel on automatic. Allow the spirit of vacation to be the filter, the lens through which you see and move through your day.

Day 6: Go someplace in your city or town where you have never been before. It may be an ethnic restaurant. Find out the specialty of the house, and order it as though you are a visitor in this new land. If you don't like it, you don't have to finish eating it, but you do have to acknowledge your willingness to be open to new experiences on your vacation. Go to a neighborhood you have never been to or haven't been to in a long time. Enjoy your vacation right where you live.

Day 7: Reflect and write your response to the following questions:

- What did you learn?
- How can you have more vacation time in your life?
- What if every day was a vacation day—how would you approach it? Do it.

WEEK 45

Listen to Music

Music is well said to be the speech of angels; in fact, nothing among the utterances allowed to man is felt to be so divine. It brings us near to the infinite.

—THOMAS CARLYLE

Listening to music is a powerful doorway to transforming your experience in the moment. Music can start your feet dancing, your body waking up, and your heart singing. A soothing instrumental can both quiet your inner experience and shift your viewpoint of your outer world. The words of a song can give you a new point of view that shifts your perspective in the moment. Music is truly a universal language that speaks directly to your spirit. Listen to it. Make it. Use it as an entryway to being wholehearted.

How to Do It

Day 1: Create a music library/playlist for yourself with an assortment of music to calm you down, lift your spirits, and get your body moving.

Day 2: Rather than mindlessly turning on the TV or getting lost in a video game or social media when you are home, make deliberate choices about the music you listen to today. When you wake up and start your day, do you want to listen to something that makes your body dance to the new day, or do you want an instrumental to slowly ease you into your new day? Maybe you would rather hear the natural music of your surroundings: birds chirping, traffic outside your window, the flush of your toilet, the flow of water through your faucet, the squeak of your closet door. Notice the instruments and the sounds of your daily life as though you are listening to an expertly composed and arranged musical masterpiece.

Day 3: Prepare and organize an assortment of music on Pandora or Spotify and pre-set radio stations in your home and car so you easily have musical choices available that feed wholehearted living.

Day 4: Experiment with listening to different kinds of music—top 40, showtunes, chanting, New Age instrumentals, rap, jazz, R&B, classical, etc. Approach this as an explorer and notice how different music influences your mood, thoughts, and experience.

Day 5: Go to a concert or invite friends to bring instruments over and make music—use spoons, pots and pans, and bottles filled with water. Play and experiment with sound.

Day 6: Sing along with the music that is playing. Your voice is an instrument; use it. Sing in the shower, hum in line at the supermarket. Notice if there is a song in your mind, and sing it. What are the words saying to you? Are they a gateway to living a life of passion and purpose, or are they telling a tale of doom and gloom? (I remember once hearing at a wedding the words "... heard it through the grapevine, not much longer would you be mine." I thought this was a very unusual choice for a wedding reception!)

Day 7: Reflect and write your response to the following questions:

- What effect does music have on you?
- What is the background music of your life?
- What is some of your favorite music?

> Music washes away from the soul the dust of everyday life.
>
> —RED AUERBACH

Experiencing music, this week, has been different than I expected. Normally it would be about the sounds made by musicians. The music for me, this week, has been about listening to the rhythms of life. The birds chirping, the breeze blowing, the sound of love from being with my friends, and being silent. The sounds of the sun shining on me and the world. I continue to deepen into my happiness.

—SHANTI GILBERT

From *Traveling Mercies: Some Thoughts on Faith*
by Anne Lamott

One of our newer [church] members, a man named Ken Nelson, is dying of AIDS, disintegrating before our very eyes. He came in a year ago with a Jewish woman who comes every week to be with us, although she does not believe in Jesus. Shortly after the man with AIDS started coming, his partner died of the disease. A few weeks later Ken told us that right after Brandon died, Jesus had slid into the hole in this heart that Brandon's loss had left, and had been there ever since. Ken has a totally lopsided face, ravaged and emaciated, but when he smiles, he is radiant. He looks like God's crazy nephew Phil. He says that he would gladly pay any price for what he has now, which is Jesus, and us.

There's a woman in the choir named Ranola who is large and beautiful and jovial and black and as devout as can be, who has been a little standoffish toward Ken. She has always looked at him with confusion, when she looks at him at all. Or she looks at him sideways, as if she wouldn't have to quite see him if she didn't look at him head on. She was raised in the South by Baptists who taught her that his way of life—that he—was an abomination. It is hard for her to break through this. I think she and a few other women at the church are, on a visceral level, a little afraid of catching the disease. But Kenny has come to church almost every week for the last year and won almost everyone over. He finally missed a couple of Sundays when he got too weak, and then a month ago he was back, weighing almost no pounds, his face even more lopsided, as if he'd had a stroke. Still, during the prayers of the people, he talked joyously of his life and his decline, of grace and redemption, of how safe and happy he feels these days.

So on this one particular Sunday, for the first hymn, the so-called Morning Hymn, we sang "Jacob's Ladder," which goes, "Every rung goes higher, higher," while ironically Kenny couldn't even stand up. But he sang away sitting down, with the hymnal in his lap. And then when it came time for the second hymn, the Fellowship Hymn, we were to sing "His Eye Is on the Sparrow." The pianist was playing and the whole congregation had risen—only Ken remained seated, holding the hymnal in his lap—and we began to sing. "Why should I feel discouraged? Why do shadows fall?" And Ranola watched Ken rather skeptically for a moment, and then her face began to melt and contort like his, and she went to his side and bent down to lift him up—lifted up this white rag doll, this scarecrow. She held him next to her, draped over and against her like a child while they sang. And it pierced me.

I can't imagine anything but music that could have brought about this alchemy. Maybe it's because music is about as physical as it gets: your essential rhythm is your heartbeat; your essential sound, the breath. We're walking temples of noise, and when you add tender heart to this mix, it somehow lets us meet in places we couldn't get to any other way.

WEEK 46

Spend Time with a Child

Children are curious and are risk takers. They have lots of courage. They venture out into a world that is immense and dangerous. A child initially trusts life and the processes of life.

—JOHN BRADSHAW

Grown men can learn from very little children for the hearts of little children are pure. Therefore, the Great Spirit may show to them many things which older people miss.

—BLACK ELK

Spending time with a child is an open doorway to the precious present. When you are in the presence of a newborn, you have a powerful reminder of the magnificent mystery and magic of life. It is interesting to note that newborns don't *do* any of the things that we as adults use to determine our worth and value. They can't feed or dress themselves. They don't have jobs or an investment portfolio. They don't have degrees or drive the newest, fastest car with the best gas mileage. They don't base their life on a to-do list or do the laundry. Yet they are reminders of what is truly the essence of life: mystery, love, wonder, possibility. As they get older, and before their domestication has them doubt themselves, they are a joy, and being with them is sometimes the best medicine for a weary soul. Asking their opinions and listening to their answers brings a lightness and simplicity to our way of thinking that opens our hearts. This week, spend time with a child—including the child within you.

How to Do It

Day 1: Notice your reaction to infants and young children today. When you walk past an infant, are you drawn to make contact? When you are in line at the supermarket or waiting for a bus, how do you react to the children you see? Do you see the magic and wonder of these "new" people? Do you automatically feel a smile on your face in the presence of children?

In 1989, I was in the Soviet Union. I spent a few hours wandering through Red Square and the surrounding streets. It was winter and gray, and the facial expressions of the people I saw also looked gray and serious. After walking many blocks, I was aware that no one was smiling, and then I saw the face of a child, the only smiling face around. I smiled and felt my spirits soar.

Day 2: Make a date to do something with a child this week, whether it is your child, your grandchildren, or your neighbor's child. Make a date and allow yourself to play, letting the child you are with be your teacher.

Day 3: Volunteer to help children. Offer to read at your local library. Volunteer to help with children in the hospital. Offer to go on a trip with your child's class. Offer to do a project in your local preschool or elementary school.

Day 4: Connect with the child in you. Find a photo of you as a child and allow your heart to open to that new being that you once were. Write a letter to your inner child, telling yourself what you appreciate about yourself. Close your eyes and remember the feeling of wonder and excitement you felt as a child. Allow your inner child to guide your way today. Allow yourself to be present in the moment and to see your everyday world through the eyes of childlike vision. Allow your inner child to play today. Get that manicure with purple glittery nail polish you have wanted for a while and were hesitant to get because you are a grown-up (or is that *groan*-up?). Have a peanut butter and jelly sandwich with the crust cut off. Allow your inner child to be your guide today.

Day 5: Get recommendations from three children on their favorite books. Go to the children's section of your local library or bookstore. Read one of the recommended books and revisit a book you loved as a child. One of my favorite books is *Ferdinand the Bull*. Just thinking about Ferdinand, I smile.

Day 6: Tell three children in your life that you love them and why they are special in your life. You can do this in person, on the phone, on a Google Hangout, or by written note, e-mail, or text. Your words of encouragement and love are powerful gifts for the children in your life. Practice this expression of care. Through expressing your love, you open yourself to the experience of love in the moment. As a responsible, loving adult, you have daily opportunities to let the children in your life know that no matter what their age, they are magnificent beings.

Day 7: Reflect and write your response to the following questions:

- What did your learn about yourself in the presence of children?
- What did you learn about yourself by connecting to your inner child?
- How can you use what you learned this week to experience a greater playfulness in your life?
- What is the most important lesson you learned this week to enhance your experience of wholehearted living?

If I Had My Child to Raise Over Again

by Diane Loomans, from *Full Esteem Ahead*

If I had my child to raise all over again,
I'd finger paint more, and point the finger less.
I'd do less correcting, and more connecting.
I'd take my eyes off my watch, and watch with my
   eyes.
I would care to know less, and know to care more.
I'd take more hikes and fly more kites.
I'd stop playing serious, and seriously play.
I would run through fields and gaze at more stars.
I'd do more hugging, and less tugging.
I would be firm less often, and affirm much more.
I'd build self-esteem first, and the house later.
I'd teach less about the love of power, and more about
   the power of love.

Children are messengers from a world we once deeply
   knew,
but we have long since forgotten.

—Alice Miller

WEEK 47

Pamper Yourself

Don't think of pampering yourself as decadence or forbidden pleasure.

Think of it as a way to preserve your sanity in an insanely paced world.

—STEPHANIE TOURLES

Pampering yourself is a requirement for sustaining wholehearted living. Sometimes there are prerequisites for courses you want to enroll in; pampering yourself is a prerequisite for greater peace and happiness in your life. Since your relationship with yourself forms the blueprint for all the relationships in your life, pampering yourself is an expression of self-love which then radiates outward, impacting all your relationships.

Most of us mean to take care of and pamper ourselves, like to do it, want to do it, but when our schedules get busy, or our finances are stretched, pampering falls by the wayside, just when we need it the most.

While pampering can be costly and time-consuming, it doesn't have to be. If you have a bathtub and running water, you can create a spa experience in your bathroom. If you have a smartphone, tablet, computer, CD player, or radio, you can surround yourself with music that soothes your soul, calms your mind, and lifts your spirit. And yes, you can go to a spa for a week surrounded by the healing embrace of nature, get daily massages, take naps, stretch your body, take some cardio-pumping hikes, and practice meditation to pamper yourself as well!

Your biggest block to pampering yourself is usually you and your habit of putting yourself last on your to-do list. This week you are number one. When you complete this prerequisite, notice peace and happiness popping up more regularly in your daily life.

How to Do It

Helpful Reading Resources:

- *2,001 Ways to Pamper Yourself* by Lorraine Bodger
- *Simple Indulgence: Easy, Everyday Things to Do for Me* by Janet Eastman
- *1,001 Ways to Relax* by Mike George
- *The Art of Living Joyfully* by Allen Klein
- *50 Simple Ways to Pamper Yourself* by Stephanie L. Tourles
- *365 Ways to Energize Mind, Body & Soul* by Stephanie L. Tourles

Day 1: Make a list of ways to pamper yourself. Each day this week, you choose one item from the list and do it—I repeat, *do it*. Here are some ideas to start your list:

- Get a massage
- Trade foot massages with a family member or friend
- Take a bubble bath
- Go to the barber and get a shave with hot shaving cream
- Get a manicure and pedicure
- Go for a walk
- Listen to great music
- Get a custom-made shirt
- Take a golf lesson
- Write in your journal
- Put a *Do Not Disturb* sign on your office or bedroom door
- Make love
- Read a novel
- Curl up and watch a movie
- Take a nap
- Meditate
- Have a cup of tea with a friend
- Use the good dishes
- Take a spa vacation
- Arrange a phone or Skype date with a dear friend
- Spend an afternoon at the movies

Days 2–6: Each day, choose an item from the list and do it. Express it this way: I have pampered myself today by:

_____

This statement is purposefully written in the past tense. Complete it in the morning as though you have already pampered yourself. Writing in the past tense is a powerful mind game that gives legs to your intention to pamper yourself. I often write items on my to-do list in the past tense, heading the list with the word *Done*. I then feel more energized, as though the items on the list are already done!

Day 7: Reflect on and write your response to the following questions:

- What did you notice by consciously pampering yourself each day?
- Make a daily pampering appointment with yourself each day for the rest of your life! Get out your calendar and schedule time for daily pampering.

WEEK 48

Wake Up to Your Faith

I tell you the truth, if you have faith as small as a
mustard seed,

you can say to this mountain, "Move from here to
there"

and it will move.

—MATTHEW 17:20

Faith in the possibility of living a life based on love,
kindness, and compassion toward yourself and others
creates the reality of this experience in your life. A
simple definition of faith is believing in something 100
percent, no conditions, no maybes, no wait and see. It is
not a question of whether or not you have faith. We all
have faith. The question is, what do you have faith in?
Do you have faith that the sun will rise each day? Do you
have faith that the tension in your marriage will never
be resolved? Where you direct your faith—consciously
and more often unconsciously—is what you create. If
you are uncertain of where you have directed your faith,

take a look at your life and your experience. Financial woes, a great job, a relationship with the love of your life, and ongoing health problems—all are reflections of what you have faith in.

There are two major categories to which you direct your faith: love or fear. If you have faith in love, in an abundant universe, in a loving God, you will view your experience through this point of view. If you put your faith in fear, focus on the worst that can happen, and gather up evidence from the past when things didn't work out, you often get to be right. Faith delivers whatever you attach it to.

Many years ago, shortly after I had moved into a new house in the midst of a divorce, I was looking forward to Thanksgiving in my new home with friends. It would be very different from the previous eleven years with my four stepchildren and my former husband's family. There would be five of us, and I saw this as a healthy way for me to embrace my new life. Shortly after midnight in the early morning hours of Thanksgiving Day, I got a call from my friend telling me that she, her husband, and daughter would not make it for Thanksgiving. I was so disappointed that I felt numb. 60 percent of my guests had just cancelled. In moments, my mind did an automatic search of all the times I had been stood up, rejected, not good enough. In the midst of this self-abuse onslaught, I said out loud, "Okay God, Loving Energy of the Universe, I know that you don't have misery in store for me. I am turning this one over to you, and I want the best Thanksgiving ever. I don't know how you're gonna do it, but I have faith that you will." I went to sleep. Thanksgiving turned out to be a glorious day, with phone calls from family, friends, and former in-laws. Another family who had invited me out for dinner came over; we ate, talked, laughed, and were grateful. I put my faith in love on that Thanksgiving Day, and the thought of it still puts a smile on my face.

Each one of us has the power to direct our faith toward the world we wish for. Each day, with news reports of war, acts of terrorism, corporate greed, constant finger-pointing and blame, it is easy to be seduced by fear. Yet everything in your world is created twice: first in your imagination, and then when it is imagined and nourished by your faith and given attention, it becomes manifest in your three-dimensional reality. You have the power to direct your faith to the possibility of your highest dreams, and trust that you can move mountains no matter what the outside circumstances are.

It seems to me that we have nothing to lose. We die anyway, so how about putting your faith in love and acting as if you live in a loving universe? You may be surprised at the love that pops up in the midst of whatever circumstances are present, like the loving phone calls on September 11 that people in the World Trade Center and on the hijacked planes made to their loved ones. This week, consciously put your faith in your dreams of a wholehearted life. Explore, experiment, and enjoy.

When you come to the edge of all the light you
    know,
And are about to step off into the darkness of
    the unknown,
Faith is knowing one of two things will happen:
There will be something solid to stand on,
Or you will be taught how to fly.

How to Do It

Day 1: Pretend that you are a computer programmer
and that today you are writing a new software program
to install in yourself. This new, state-of-the-art, always
upgradable program is called *Where I Put My Faith.*
Write your program. Here are some of mine:

- I have faith in a loving universe.
- I have faith that my prayers are answered.
- I have faith that I can trust the guidance of my
  heart.
- I have faith that all circumstances are either an
  expression of love or a call for love.

Day 2: Practice the **F.A.I.T.H.** acronym:

- F: Feel what you are feeling.
- A: Acknowledge the truth of who you are: an
  expression of the Loving Energy of the Universe.
- I: Invite your consciousness to be aware of love's

presence in all situations and circumstances in your life and in yourself.

- T: Trust love's presence in your life—the still small voice—that your prayers are heard and are being answered.
- H: Honor every moment as a precious gift.

Day 3: Identify something you desire. Every time it pops into your mind, see it as accomplished. You want financial abundance? Use your imagination to see your bank balance on your next statement reading $3,000,000.00. You don't have to figure out how this will happen. Allow your faith to illuminate the path to your desire. When you get too focused on *how* it should happen, you limit the possibilities of the mysterious and miraculous ways of the co-creative process. Remember to acknowledge anything that comes into your life that represents abundance, even a penny you find on the street! Make sure that in your imagery of seeing your desire fulfilled, you experience yourself feeling happy, satisfied, and prosperous.

Day 4: Witness yourself today. Notice where you put your faith. If your beliefs are not supporting what you desire, change them and charge your new thoughts with your conviction—your faith. I was in a horrendous traffic jam one holiday weekend. I had been sitting in the traffic for about three minutes, which felt like an eternity, since my faith automatically became wedded to being in traffic for the next few hours. I was imagining my three-hour drive turning into a very long five-hour expedition. After a while of feeling victimized by the traffic, I noticed what I was doing and had a new thought. I saw myself arriving at my destination, saying to my friends, "I had a great, easy ride here. The roads were clear and here I am, on time!" Within moments I was feeling relaxed, noticing the scenery, and the next thing I knew the traffic had cleared. I had put my faith in a new thought and I changed my experience.

You may be thinking, "This is just a traffic story. What about when something serious is going on?" I have heard two separate stories from friends who were mugged. In each of these cases, somewhere in the midst of the horror, they were able to change the focus of their attention. One person started singing a chant that calmed him. Within moments, the bandits who had broken into and were now driving his car stopped the car, apologized, and said they wouldn't hurt anyone. In another story, a woman was in the vestibule of an apartment building in New York City waiting for the buzzer to let her into the lobby of the building. Someone came up behind her and grabbed her, telling her to give him her money and not to scream. She was afraid. Time slowed down, and as she was reaching up to hand her purse to him she started saying, in her mind, "I love you, I love you, I love you." The next thing she knew he let her go and ran out of the building, without her purse.

Day 5: Write a poem or essay about faith.

Day 6: Direct your faith to the possibility of heaven on earth. See heaven on earth as you move through your day. At the end of the day, make a list of all the examples of heaven on earth you saw and experienced today. Some examples of heaven on earth for me are:

- Flowers
- A laughing child
- A hug
- My dog running on the beach
- A customer service person easily solving my problem
- A friend's smile
- The taste of a sweet, fresh strawberry
- Cars pulling over to let an emergency vehicle pass
- The abundance of fresh food at the farmers' market
- Spooning in the morning with a lover

Have faith in heaven on earth; see heaven on earth and it will expand.

Day 7: Reflect on and write your response to the following questions:

- What did you learn?
- What is the faith program that is now "running" you?
- What is your plan for when you notice that your faith in love is wavering?

> Take the first step in faith.
> You don't have to see the whole staircase,
> just take the first step.
> —MARTIN LUTHER KING, JR.

WEEK 49

Harness the Power
of Your Imagination

> We use our imagination 48 percent of the time and
> so you've got to be aware of that. If you spend your
> time worrying and being fearful about what's coming,
> instead of dreaming about what you'd like to see
> coming, you shift your attention to things you want
> less of. You want to keep your attention on things you
> want more of.
>
> — PATTI DOBROWOLSKI

When you consciously harness the full resources of your
imagination in support of living a wholehearted life of
passion and purpose, you are taking responsibility for
your role in the creative process.

One of the fascinating aspects of being human is
that the things you focus your attention on expand
in your experience. You don't actually have to be in a
particular situation to experience its impact. You can
simply imagine it. Create a virtual reality of a circumstance using the full resources of your imagination—
activating all of your senses—and it is as if you are
having the experience. For example, you are on vaca-

tion, lounging on a comfortable chair near the water's edge. You hear the sound of the turquoise surf lapping against the shore. You smell the subtle hint of salt in the air. You feel the warmth of the sun combined with a gentle breeze caressing your body. Your head is turned slightly to the right and you see your lover in the chair beside you. Close your eyes for a moment and imagine this scene. Open your eyes and notice how you feel right now, having imagined this beach scene.

Suddenly, the thought of the pressures and demands of home and work enters your mind and hooks your attention. Immediately you feel tightness in your shoulders and butterflies in your stomach, and the words in your mind sound something like, "Oh, no. I don't want to go back to work." A feeling of dissatisfaction and unhappiness fills your being. Even when you are still on the beach and your physical environment has remained pleasurable, your focus on a different virtual reality—a daydream—transformed your experience.

When you truly understand the profound life-changing power you have available to you at each and every moment simply by where you focus your attention, you can experience greater peace and happiness every day.

Most of us have learned to focus on what is missing or lacking in our lives. Have you ever noticed that when you are happy, you frequently expect that it won't last long, or that something will happen to ruin it? When you harness the power of your imagination to create pleasurable experiences that reflect your dreams and goals, you are actually creating the blueprint that will nourish your desired results. When experiences of lack, fear, hell, and suffering capture your attention, you can acknowledge them and move through them with greater ease. Remember, in your virtual reality, you are not focusing on how your goal will be achieved; rather, you are experiencing a scene that is a reflection of your dream accomplished.

It is crucial that you not judge yourself when fear, anger, lack, and hell take center stage in your life. Old patterns operate on automatic. It takes attention and discipline, over time, to create new patterns of thought and behavior—new brain pathways. Fear, anger, lack, and suffering are powerful calls for love in your life. It is not that you are bad for feeling them. These feelings are a reminder that you are at a growing edge, a leading edge that doesn't have to be a bleeding edge in your life. These feelings are your personal guidance system, letting you know that your connection with Loving Source Energy is constricted. Rather than being seduced by the dramatic interpretation that you are attaching to the situation, the best place to focus your attention is on getting centered, transforming your energetic frequency through expanding your connection with the Loving Energy of the Universe.

Harnessing the full resources of your imagination allows you to practice having thoughts that create good feelings and to become proficient at transforming your experience in the moment. Creating a virtual reality is a potent tool to have in your toolbox to envision your heart's desire and to *see* your most heartfelt image for well-being in every situation you step into. This week you will consciously hone your expertise as a virtual reality creator. Remember, the only limits are those you allow, so lead with your heart and trust in the possibility of your dreams.

How to Do It

Day 1: Make a Pleasure List. This is a list of the people, places, things, and activities that, when you focus your attention on them, give you a sense of well-being, happiness, contentment—pleasure (first introduced to a Pleasure List during Week 1). To deepen your experience of your Pleasure List choose one item on your list, and once an hour for thirty seconds, use your imagination to create a virtual reality of it. Here's how:

- Close your eyes and imagine an item on your pleasure list.
- Place yourself in the scene. Be specific; include where you are, the time of day, what you are wearing, etc.
- Experience your virtual reality with all of your senses—sight, hearing, touch, taste, and smell.

If at any time during these thirty seconds you feel anything other than pleasure, get out of the scene you are imagining, open your eyes, take a conscious deep breath, and start again. It is helpful to start with scenes that don't involve other people, since we often have a tendency to bring others into our virtual reality whom we want to change and fix—for their own good, of course! The purpose of this exercise is to give you practice feeling good, *not* to fix people or circumstances in your life.

Day 2: Repeat Day 1. You can use the same item from your Pleasure List, or a different one.

Day 3: During the day, whenever you notice that hell is flirting with you, use the full resources of your imagination to create a pleasurable thirty-second virtual reality, using the technique from Day 1. You may be able to unhook and detach energetically after thirty seconds, or you may have to consciously, repeatedly engage your imagination. Remember, this is a practice in changing where you focus your attention and thereby your experience in the present moment. Once you are feeling centered, you will be more open and able to move through whatever circumstances are present.

Day 4: Using the technique from Day 1, five times today, harness the power of your imagination to daydream— to visualize—a big dream. *See* your big dream accomplished. Savor it, taste it, feel it, and know that the universe is saying a resounding *Yes*.

Day 5: Use virtual reality to *see* every situation you are stepping into as fully and completely satisfying. For instance, as you are getting out of bed in the morning, *see* yourself stepping out of the shower feeling refreshed, alert, clean, and eager for a new love-filled day. As you get ready to leave your house in the morning, *see* yourself arriving at your destination safely, having enjoyed the journey. Play with this, have fun, and enjoy your day.

Day 6: Practice consciously engaging your imagination throughout the day, once an hour and whenever you want to transform hell to heaven. Strengthen your new habit of tapping into the infinite resources of your imagination to uplift your experience and set your direction throughout the day.

Day 7: Reflect and write your response to the following questions:

- What did you learn about your imagination this week?
- What was most surprising to you?
- How can you keep this muscle strong and toned? Do it.

Limitations live only in our minds. But if we use our imagination, our possibilities become limitless.

—JAMIE PAOLINETTI

You see things; and you say "Why?" But I dream things that never were; and I say, "Why not?"

—GEORGE BERNARD SHAW

WEEK 50

Enjoy a Massage

If you "don't have time" for a massage, you may be the one who needs it the most.

—LAHEY CLINIC

Massage is a glorious form of touch that releases tension, fosters a deeper connection with your body, and offers the nourishment of loving touch. Often in our daily life there are many taboos regarding touch. The danger of sexual harassment accusations stops us from reaching out and massaging a coworker's shoulders in the midst of a stressful workday. Have you ever held back from asking for a massage for fear that you will be misunderstood to be making a sexual innuendo? Sometimes when we are receiving a massage, we are shy about saying "Harder" or "Softer," and when we are giving a massage, we question our competence. These are some reasons that massage may be outside of your everyday activities. While a massage is definitely special, when it is incorporated into your daily life, your well-being surges and peace and happiness abound.

While there are many different kinds of massage for which people attend school and are licensed, you can benefit from receiving and giving a massage to a family member, lover, or friend even without receiving formal training. I often think of the stories I read in my college psychology textbook about the importance of physical touch for orphaned infants. Studies were reported that demonstrated that infants who received only minimal touch would not grow and develop normally and would sometimes die. They were starved for touch.

As an adult, you continue to have the same need for physical connection. Massage is a form of touch that provides this connection and soothes your body. Massage creates the opportunity to move your attention outside of your head (which for most of us is overused) and to feel with your magnificent sensory system, your body. When you experience regular connection with your body, you are better able to utilize the guidance system of your physical sensations to alert you to whether you are in heaven or hell.

This week, give and receive massage and notice the effect of this simple act of touch on your life.

How to Do It

Day 1: Give your feet a massage today. Get some special oil or some foot massage lotion, or use some body oil you have in the house, and lovingly massage your feet. Imagine that these are the feet of your beloved (aren't they?) and you are thanking them for all they do for you. Your feet carry you around all day, bearing the full weight of your body, sometimes squeezed into shoes that look better than they feel! Massage each toe, feel it, look at it. You may even say the poem from childhood: *This little piggy went to market*, and so on. Notice what your skin looks and feels like, where it is soft and smooth, where it is rough. Savor this glorious touch, and then move on to your other foot. To get the full benefit of your massage, do it in silence or with some relaxing music on so you can focus your attention on giving and receiving this loving massage. Spend a minimum of ten minutes on each foot. When you are finished massaging, put on a pair of cozy cotton socks. Notice how your feet feel and how *you* feel.

Day 2: Make an appointment for a massage this week. If this is something you do regularly, make an appointment for a different kind of massage than usual. If this is something you have never done before, ask family and friends for their suggestions or call a spa or yoga center in your area for information and help in choosing what kind of massage to get and where to get it. You may also do research online to get descriptions of different kinds of massage (some forms of massage are Swedish, Shiatsu, Reflexology, Sports, and Trager). Massage schools are often looking for bodies to work on; check to see if there is a massage school in your area.

Sign up for a massage class. There are classes for individuals and couples. Check your local Y, community education programs, and yoga centers for this information. There is also a wealth of information about massage on YouTube, in your local library, and in bookstores.

Day 3: Give and receive three shoulder massages today. Ask family or friends if they'd like to do a shoulder massage trade. This can be as short as two minutes each, standing up; or longer with the receiver sitting down and the giver standing behind the receiver. When you are the masseuse, ask the receiver to let you know what feels good, if she or he wants it harder or softer, higher or lower. It is helpful to be silent other than when you are asking for and getting feedback. As the giver, allow yourself to focus your attention fully on what you are doing and feeling. I have found that when I allow the silence, my fingers often sense where to massage. When you finish giving the shoulder massage, shake the energy out of your hands. When you are the receiver, you may want to experiment with feeling what "harder" and "softer" feel like. Trust the cues of your body to let you know what feels good.

Be aware that if you have not experienced regular bodywork, you may be more sensitive than you expected. Our bodies hold our tension and the traumas and dramas of our past. Sometimes when you are touched, a sore spot that has been tight for months or years will be very sensitive to touch, both physically and emotionally. The shoulder massages you are exchanging today are for relaxation.

Often when I lead stress management workshops in corporate or business settings, at some point in the workshop, I instruct participants to form a circle and massage the shoulders of the person in front of them (first asking for permission to touch), and then turn around to massage the person who just massaged them. There is often laughter, since this is so different from business as usual in the workplace, as well as sighs of pleasant feelings.

Day 4: Get a quick massage today. There are many nail salons that offer short shoulder and neck chair massages for women and men (ten minutes for ten dollars). In some cities, malls also offer chair massages that charge by the minute. I know of some businesses that provide this kind of chair massage as part of their employee wellness program. Sometimes the employer pays, sometimes the employee pays, and sometimes they split the fee. If you are a boss or own a business, you may want to look into this as a treat for your employees, whether it's one day, once a week, once a month, or during a particularly stressful time at work.

Day 5: When you get out of the shower or bath today, massage your body with oil or body lotion. So often we automatically get out of the shower or bath, quickly dry ourselves, possibly use body lotion, get dressed, and move on to our next activity. Today, if you have the news or even music blaring, turn it off, and massage your body in silence as an act of love and appreciation. Feel what the skin feels like on different parts of your body. Know that the oil or moisturizing lotion you are using, combined with your loving touch, is nourishing your body. Did you know that your skin is your largest organ? It is constantly exposed to heat and cold and all different types of fabrics. Honor your skin today, pay attention to it, nourish it as you massage your body slowly and carefully.

Day 6: Trade a massage with a family member, friend, or lover. It may be a full body massage, a foot massage, back and shoulders—you decide.

Day 7: Reflect and write your response to the following questions:

- What did you learn this week by focusing on giving and receiving massages?
- What was your experience giving? Receiving?
- How did massage contribute to your well being?
- How can you incorporate massage into your life?

> The body never lies.
>
> — MARTHA GRAHAM

WEEK 51

Be the World's Greatest Lover

All mankind loves a lover.

—RALPH WALDO EMERSON

Being the world's greatest lover is the leading role you were meant to play in this life. While the idea of the world's greatest lover may initially evoke images of a Don Juan or a current-day Marilyn Monroe, I mean to include people who express love in all they think, say, and do. Since the essence of who you are is love (God is love, you are made in the image of God; therefore, you are love, and we are each a mighty expression of love), each one of us has the potential to be the world's greatest lover. As a great lover, you can express your love through your sexuality as well as in your own unique way, in all that you think, all that you say, and all that you do. When you allow loving energy, Source Energy, to flow through you, everything that is not love, including anger, jealousy, envy, and guilt, dissolves. Love is the force, the power that transforms everything in its path.

Too often in our lives, we put our energy and our attention into doing things, fixing things, curing things. Yet the starting point of transforming any experience is always the presence of love, allowing Source Energy to move through your being, entering your body with every inhalation and leaving your body with every exhalation, entering your mind with every thought you give attention to and contributing to the collective consciousness of the universe through your thoughts and words. Your feelings are your personal guidance system, notifying you when you are in sync with the flow of love and when there is a need for you to focus and expand your capacity for love, during those times that fear, anger, resentment, and worry have surfaced.

This week, act as if you are the world's greatest lover, and offer your love in all situations and to all people who cross your path—including yourself. If you forget that being the world's greatest lover is the role you were born to play, as soon as you remember, step into that role again, loving yourself through it all. Remember, being the world's greatest lover is another name for living a wholehearted life.

How to Do It

Movies to watch and notice what happens to the characters in the presence of love:

- *Beauty and the Beast* (Disney)
- *Don Juan DeMarco*

- *Edward Scissorhands*
- *Groundhog Day*
- *Happy*
- *Her*
- *I Am*
- *Life as a House*
- *Life Is Beautiful*
- *Shrek*

Day 1: Sit quietly and allow the idea of being the world's greatest lover to fill your being. You may notice sexy, graceful, sensual, affectionate images coming to mind. As this happens, allow your body and your being to be transformed. Feel the idea of being the world's greatest lover come alive in you. When this idea fills your being, easily and gently open your eyes and see the world from the vantage point of being the world's greatest lover. Repeat this exercise once an hour and notice how you feel, how you move, how you express yourself from this vantage point.

Day 2: Write an essay entitled "I Am the World's Greatest Lover." Read this every day and live it.

Day 3: Imagine that the greatest sin ("sin" meaning being off the mark in your connection with God, with Source Energy) in the world is not expressing your love; that the greatest abuse you inflict on yourself and others is withholding your love. With that in mind, be free of sin today and express your love as the world's greatest lover.

Day 4: Make a list of the people you think are the world's greatest lovers. Next to each person's name, write the quality of love they express; then, act as if you have those qualities. Here are some of mine:

- My mother—unconditional love for me
- Solange, my granddaughter—joy in discovering new things
- Rhone, my grandson—strong hugs
- Mother Teresa—compassion
- Martin Luther King, Jr.—the power of a big dream
- don Miguel Ruiz—loving hugs and wisdom
- Jesus—a forgiving heart; seeing everyone and everything as an expression of God
- The Dalai Lama—a contagious smile
- Antonio Banderas—sex appeal
- Meryl Streep—beauty and talent

Day 5: Say "I love you" in your thoughts to every person you see or speak with today. This includes people you see on TV, in the subway, at the supermarket. Notice how you feel doing this. Remember, this is unconditional, independent of any of this person's actions or circumstances. This includes the person talking too loudly on her cell phone; the executive who stole from his company; the trusted adult who abuses a child.

Day 6: Create a collage that represents yourself as the world's greatest lover. Hang it where you can see it, and let the images of this self-portrait fill your being.

Day 7: Reflect on and write your responses to the following questions:

- What did you learn about yourself?
- How can you continue to be the world's greatest lover?

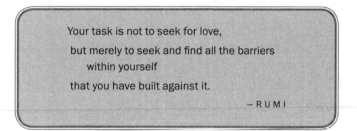

Your task is not to seek for love,

but merely to seek and find all the barriers within yourself

that you have built against it.

—RUMI

WEEK 52
Celebrate Success

The Successful Self feels valuable, self-accepting and
self-confident.

—DOROTHY ROWE

Focusing on success has two components. The first is
how you define success, and the second is where you
place your attention. Most if not all of us have grown
up focusing on outside measures of success: getting an
"A" on a report card, winning a game, living a socially
acceptable life (i.e., marriage, children, good job, and
nice home). Yet many people have had these successes
and have not experienced peace of mind and joy. A
wholehearted life requires a definition of success that is
aligned with who you are. Like happiness, it is an inside
job that begins with listening to your heart's desire,
knowing your purpose and dreams, and honoring your

integrity. It is through this experience of being whole and aligned in your inner and outer life that you truly experience success.

Your ideas and beliefs about yourself are the foundation of whether or not you experience success. If you are judgmental, self-abusive, or filled with regret and shame, no matter what you achieve in the outside world, you will not feel successful. If you are self-accepting and loving, you will experience success each step of the way, honoring the journey and appreciating the destination.

In 1999 I had a powerful experience of success. I had been diagnosed with uterine fibroids many years before. After a variety of treatments and remedies, my acupuncturist encouraged me to schedule surgery. I decided that I would approach this with all the tools I would suggest to others. I chose a great surgeon and had a session with a psychologist who uses hypnosis to prepare patients for an easy surgery and quick recovery. I listened to audio tapes (this was before mp3s!) describing the skills and expertise of my surgical team and my easy, quick, and comfortable recuperation. I asked the anesthesiologist to whisper in my ear at the end of the procedure that the surgery had been a success and that I would heal easily and completely. I asked family and friends to pray for my highest good and the highest good of my surgical team. On the day of the surgery, I felt calm and confident, focusing my attention on seeing myself in my home and feeling comfortable. And that is exactly what happened. I went home two days after surgery, my recuperation was easy, and my surgeon commented on how quickly I recovered.

This doesn't mean that this is a prescription you should follow when facing surgery. Rather, it is a reminder that in being true to ourselves and in marching to our own drummer, we create the opportunity for success. By concentrating on healing and using the complementary medicine that I had faith in, I focused on success.

This week, explore how you define success, experiment with broadening your definition, and, through your focus on success, enjoy the gifts in your life.

How to Do It

Day 1: Explore what you believe about success through the following exercise.

1. Complete the following statements. (Allow all responses and freely associate.)
   - Success is _____
   - I am successful when I _____

2. After you complete your list, put a check mark next to beliefs that support you in being successful, and cross out each belief that hinders your success.

3. Use your check marked statements as affirmations (thoughts that you affirm by repetition). Each morning and evening, read your affirmations aloud and feel the power of the words fill your being. If you hear and notice contradictory thoughts entering your mind, take a deep breath and say, "Thanks for sharing and I choose..." Restate your affirmation with conviction and authority. Remember, you are the author of your beliefs.

Day 2: Make a Success List. On a piece of paper, in your appointment book, or on your computer, tablet, or smartphone, make a list of your successes as they occur during the day. Read your list aloud at night and allow yourself to experience your success. If you are judgmental or abusive as you read the list, go back to the beginning and read it again until you can go through the entire list and feel successful.

Day 3: Brag about your success. Have success conversations, tell three people about your experience focusing on success, and share your success on social media.

Day 4: Make a collage of what success means to you, and remember to include yourself in the collage—this is *your* success story. Place your collage in a prominent spot, on your refrigerator or a wall filled with art made by the children in your life. When you are asked about it, tell your success story.

Day 5: Repeat the exercise from Day 1, making adjustments to your affirmations if necessary. Randomly write your affirmations in your calendar and on the top of each page or every few pages of your journal. Put a sticky note with an affirmation on it inside your closet door or in your underwear drawer. Fill your house, office, and car with your affirmations; put them in places you don't see daily so you will be surprised when you see them and they catch your attention. These are reminders to focus on success.

Day 6: Write a love letter to yourself about focusing on success. You may include what success is to you, a list of your successes, or reminders to keep you focused on success. Put the letter in an envelope, seal and stamp it, and give it to a friend or family member. Ask this person to mail the letter back to you within the next one to two months so it will be a pleasant surprise when it arrives at the most perfect time.

Day 7: Reflect on and write your response to the following questions:

- What you have learned about focusing on success?
- What obstacles to focusing on success did you notice?
- What are your patterns of thoughts and beliefs that block your awareness of success? (Knowing these thought patterns is very powerful. When they pop up, simply say "Oops" and choose a different train of thought to board.)
- How does focusing on success contribute to your peace of mind and happiness?
- What was your most important insight this week?

Putting It All Together—
Creating a Bag of Tricks

When all is said and done, each one of us is truly a
bag of tricks—
A magical, mysterious creation.

A bag of tricks is a pouch filled with good luck charms
that serve as reminders of the qualities that you may
forget you always have access to. In some Native American cultures medicine bags or medicine bundles contain
a collection of items that represent the "medicine" or
power the wearer wants to have or amplify.

Since living a wholehearted life requires that you
have access to and consciously direct your personal
power it is helpful to have a bag of tricks to fill with
lucky charms and reminders of the techniques and
qualities that support a life of passion, purpose, and
authenticity. In a sense this book is a bag of tricks; it

is filled with ideas and techniques that are entryways—portals—to the sacred marriage of body mind spirit. The more you practice the exercises and use the ideas, the easier it will be for you to consciously choose Love as the energy through which you experience life. It is quite possible though, that you may not carry this book with you always! In that case a special pouch that you fill with your lucky charms can always be nearby for you to see, touch, feel, and open. And in the process be reminded of the power, the perspective that is always available to you for the choosing.

In addition to actually having a bag of tricks, a pouch filled with power objects, you may already have lucky charms with you that you touch and reach for, sometimes without even being aware that you are doing that, in times of stress. Are you wearing or do you, right now, have with you a lucky charm, is there one nearby, or has one been popping into your mind as you've been reading these words? That special penny that you always keep in your wallet; the watch that belonged to your great-grandfather and was passed on to you by your father; the rabbit foot that you keep in your sock drawer that was given to you by your favorite aunt when you were a child and now whenever you notice it you gently stroke it and feel loved and safe; that special outfit you always wear when you fly on an airplane; your wedding band that reminds you each time you look at it that love is more important than being right in your marriage; that lucky tee, that's chipped now, that you always carry in your pocket that you believe brings you good luck on the golf course.

We can endow things with qualities and energy so they evoke a vibration, a frequency, energy within us, or we can fill our pouch with items that are believed to have a particular meaning and vibration, and through our faith in their power they activate a particular vibration within us. For instance the Native American Crow tribe believed that an elk tooth was medicine that would bring material abundance to its owner and a piece of blue cloth meant good luck.

In addition to these good luck charms we also call upon saints, angels, and fairies at different times in our lives to guide our way. Remember the enchanting power of the tooth fairy? So, this week, in the spirit of putting it all together create your own bag of tricks, use it and you will notice as time goes by that thoughts of your lucky charms will pop into your mind at the most perfect time and serve as regular companions and reminders for you to live your life through a foundation of love.

How to Do It

Day 1–Day 4: Make a list of the kind of medicine, power, and qualities you want to have easy access to. Some of you items on your list may be:

Health
Abundance
Patience
Acceptance of self and others
Peace
Love
Sense of humor
Loving relationships

When you have completed your list (and remember you can always make changes to it) choose items that represent each of the qualities. One way to do this is to close your eyes, focus on the quality, and ask yourself the following question: *What is a symbol of this quality?* And listen to the answer. (It is possible that you may not immediately get a clear answer, that's okay—you may choose to write the quality on a small piece of paper and trust that the perfect symbol will reveal itself to you.)

On Day 5 you are going to make your bag of tricks with the items you have gathered. You can use a pouch that you make, buy, or already have. This may be something you choose to wear around your neck, carry in your pocket or purse, or place on your altar. If you are going to make it, choose material and cut and sew a pouch. Be creative, and remember you can only do this right. (I carry a black velvet bag of tricks in my purse. It is made from a pair of pants that had worn out, it is a bit lopsided and my sewing is primitive, and whenever I see it, touch it, think of it, open it, I feel as though I am with a dear friend.)

Day 5: Make your bag of tricks. Approach this as a sacred activity. Gather all the items you'll need for your bag of tricks; you may put on some lovely music, light a candle or two and, before you jump into the task of doing, prepare yourself by following these instructions:

Take a deep breath, inhaling and exhaling, and close your eyes.

Focus on your breath as you feel your body mind become more relaxed and more at ease.

When you experience yourself fully present in your body, state your intention: *I choose to create a bag of tricks that will support me in living a wholehearted life. Each symbol I place in my pouch will be a reminder of the qualities that I always have access to.*

Open your eyes and say aloud the *Prayer for Whole-hearted Living* (page xxx).

Now it is time to place each item in your bag. Hold each item in your hands one at a time (even if it is simply a piece of paper with the quality written on it). As you hold it feel the quality it represents, breathe that quality into it as you exhale and as you inhale receive that quality from the item. Make an agreement with each power object, asking it to remind you of this quality when you forget and that you will use its reminder and connect with the quality. After you have made the agreement, place your power symbol in your pouch until you have agreements with each item in your pouch. You now have a bag of tricks, a medicine bag. Use it, listen to it, and if you ever get the impulse to add items or remove items do it.

Day 6: Anytime during the day when you feel off center or in need of extra support take out your bag of tricks and ask for the help you need; if you are unclear on what you need, ask for guidance and then reach into your bag and trust that whichever power object you get is an answer to your need and allow its quality to fill you and illuminate your way.

Day 7: Write your reflections on creating a bag of tricks:

- What was this experience like for you?
- How can you use your bag of tricks?
- What did you learn?
- What other power objects and symbols do you have and use?

Sometimes you might need to take something out of your medicine bag. I used to have a red stone, but it turned black after awhile. My great-grandmother told me to take that stone out because it has taken on the negative energy and it was time to replace it.

—DUANE WATKINS

My Pocket Angel

One morning when Mom was in the intensive care unit, two months before her death, I handed her a Pocket Angel—a coin-sized, pewter charm with a love angel on it—and asked her to bless it. I told her I would always carry it with me and this way she would always be close to me, my special angel. It's in my wallet. I see it and touch it when I get change. Thinking of it and touching it evoke the loving embrace of Mom. It truly is a lucky charm.

Afterword

As I write this, there is much unrest in the world. Terrorists in Iraq and Syria are on a rampage. A cease-fire between Israelis and Palestinians is fragile. The Ebola virus continues to claim lives in Africa. Climate change is evident in changing weather patterns. As the rich get richer the middle class continues to disappear. In the USA partisan politics focuses on blame, finger-pointing, and name-calling as corporations wield their wealth and influence in service of their self-interests.

While there are times that I feel overwhelmed and hopeless in the face of violence and hatred, with decades of practice of consciously choosing to live a wholehearted life, I view all of this misery as a call for love. Since I believe that everything that exists begins in consciousness—I see that I do have a crucial part to play in contributing to a more peaceful and loving world.

My part is to be loving. To appreciate that at each and every moment each one of us is doing the very best we can, based on our programming—our beliefs. With this in mind, my work—where I place my energy—is to cultivate an attitude and a way of being that is a reflec-tion of compassion, kindness, forgiveness, and love. There are times that I am better at this than others.

Yet, when I remember that each moment is a new beginning and each breath offers a new opportunity, I feel empowered.

Your thoughts, your energy, and your Love are potent forces that contribute to the collective consciousness. And the truth is that we don't know whose energy will be the tipping point that transforms partisanship into cooperation, resentment and anger into forgiveness, and hopelessness into hopefulness.

For decades I've wondered, *What is all the fighting for?* We all die anyway. Why not feast on the glorious opportunity life on earth offers us? It sure sounds simple enough. But until there is peace, joy, and love alive in each one of us this is not so simple. What I know for sure is that you will be confronted with challenges, disappointments, and dreams that feel bigger than you. And that when your fears and worries surface it may seem that all this "stuff" that I've written about is just that, "stuff." Yet, it is in these moments that the call for love is actually the loudest—and because you are reading these words, I trust that you have heard, and are hearing, the call.

I am grateful, hopeful, and filled with love that you have joined me on this journey to live a wholehearted life. Remember, everything in creation begins as an idea in our imagination. And then, when an idea is wedded with faith, spoken of with authority, and acted on with conviction, miracles—even the miracle of peace—are possible.

Much of writing is a solitary process—and while I do often talk with family, friends, and colleagues about my ideas and get their feedback, now that this book is in your hands, I would love to know

what works for you, what you discovered, and questions you have. So feel free to contact me directly at
Susyn@SusynReeve.com.

September 17, 2014
The Berkshires

Resources

Here is a list of some of my favorite books and below I have listed resources for specific chapters:

Daring Greatly: How the Courage to Be Vulnerable Transforms the Way We Live, Love, Parent, and Lead—Brene Brown

Imperfect Spirituality: Extraordinary Enlightenment for Ordinary People—Polly Campbell

Constructive Wallowing: How to Beat Bad Feelings By Letting Yourself Have Them—Tina Gilbertson

Having the Time of Your Life: Little Lessons to Live By—Allen Klein

The Grateful Table: Blessings, Prayers and Graces for the Daily Meal—Brenda Knight

What Are You Waiting For?: Learn How to Rise to the Occasion of Your Life—Kristen Moeller

Reduced to Joy—Mark Nepo

The Four Agreements: A Practical Guide to Personal Freedom—don Miguel Ruiz

SQ 21: The Twenty-One Skills of Spiritual Intelligence—Cindy Wigglesworth

Week 16. Write Down Your Soul
Writing Down Your Soul—Janet Conner

Week 17. Adorn Yourself
In Your Element: Showing Up As Your Essential Self
(http://bit.ly/BarbaraCarroll)

Week 19. Meditate
The Benefits of Meditation and Guided Visualizations
(http://bit.ly/2Meditate)

Week 23. Live Abundantly
Money, Love and Purpose: Healing the Rift (http://bit.
ly/FinancialAlchemy)

Week 31. Take a Risk
The Power of Vulnerability TED Talk by Brene Brown
(http://bit.ly/TEDTalkVulnerability)

Week 35. Seize the Moment—Be Here Now
Be Here Now—Ram Dass
The Power of Now—Eckhart Tolle
Groundhog Day—Columbia Pictures

Week 40. Pray
 The Way We Pray: Celebrating Spirit from Around the
World

Week 41. Detach and Let Go
"Let It Go" from Frozen (http://bit.ly/LetItGoSong)
Cutting the Strings Guided Visualization (http://bit.ly/
CutTheStrings)
Transforming Negative Thoughts Video (http://bit.ly/
TransformNegativeThoughts)

Week 42. Eat Dessert First
Great Recipes (http://elissagoodman.com/recipes/)

Week 44. Take a Vacation
Most Relaxing Scene Visualization (http://bit.ly/Relax-
    ingScene)

Permissions

An exhaustive effort has been made to clear all reprint permissions for this book. If any required acknowledgment has been omitted, it is unintentional. If notified, the publishers will be pleased to rectify any omission in future editions.

The author gratefully acknowledges permission to use the following material:

"The Breath Is Life's Teacher" by Donna Martin (www. donnamartin.net) used by permission of the author.

"Over the Rainbow," by Harold Arlen and E.Y. Harburg © 1938 (Renewed 1966) Metro-Goldwn-Mayer Inc. © 1939 (Renewed in 1967) EMI Feist Catalog Inc. All Rights Reserved. Used by Permissions of WARNER BROS. PUBLICATIONS U.S. INC., Miami, FL.

"Miracles" Excerpt from *Traveling Mercies* by Anne Lamott, copyright © 1999 Anne Lamott. Used by permission of Pantheon Books, a division of Random House, Inc.

"Autobiography in Five Short Chapters" from *There's*

About Susyn

 SUSYN REEVE has forty years of experience as a self-esteem expert, master coach, corporate consultant, interfaith minister and award-winning author. Yet the title that best captures her wholehearted life is GodMother. As a teen, she wrote in her journal, *"What would the world be like if everyone loved themselves?"* This question informs her commitment to partner with clients and guide them in deepening and expanding their capacity to experience vibrant self-esteem and success in all arenas of their lives. She has been a delegate to the UN Commission on the Status of Women and an adjunct Associate Professor of Management at New York University focusing on Leadership and Interpersonal and Group Dynamics. She is a member of the New Thought Center of Eastern Long Island and is one of the ministers offering the Sunday Service message. Follow Susyn's blog and learn about her work at www.SusynReeve.com and listen to the On Purpose Radio Show she co-hosts at www.OnPurposeShow.com.

to our readers

Viva Editions publishes books that inform, enlighten, and entertain. We do our best to bring you, the reader, quality books that celebrate life, inspire the mind, revive the spirit, and enhance lives all around. Our authors are practical visionaries: people who offer deep wisdom in a hopeful and helpful manner. Viva was launched with an attitude of growth and we want to spread our joy and offer our support and advice where we can to help you live the Viva way: vivaciously!

We're grateful for all our readers and want to keep bringing you books for inspired living. We invite you to write to us with your comments and suggestions, and what you'd like to see more of. You can also sign up for our online newsletter to learn about new titles, author events, and special offers.

Viva Editions
2246 Sixth St.
Berkeley, CA 94710
www.vivaeditions.com
(800) 780-2279
Follow us on Twitter @vivaeditions
Friend/fan us on Facebook